Philosophies of Communication

PETER LANG
New York • Washington, D.C./Baltimore • Bern
Frankfurt am Main • Berlin • Brussels • Vienna • Oxford

Philosophies of Communication

Implications for Everyday Experience

Melissa A. Cook & Annette M. Holba

EDITORS

PETER LANG
New York • Washington, D.C./Baltimore • Bern
Frankfurt am Main • Berlin • Brussels • Vienna • Oxford

Library of Congress Cataloging-in-Publication Data

Philosophies of communication: implications for everyday experience /
[edited by] Melissa A. Cook, Annette M. Holba.
p. cm.
Includes bibliographical references and index.
1. Communication—Philosophy. I. Cook, Melissa A.
II. Holba, Annette.
P90.P46   302.201—dc22   2008006207
ISBN-13: 978-1-4331-0219-6 (hardcover)
ISBN 978-1-4331-0220-2 (paperback)

Bibliographic information published by **Die Deutsche Bibliothek**.
Die Deutsche Bibliothek lists this publication in the "Deutsche
Nationalbibliografie"; detailed bibliographic data is available
on the Internet at http://dnb.ddb.de/.

Cover design by Clear Point Designs
Cover photo of Annette Holba, © Bill Laprade, Laprade Studio 2007

The paper in this book meets the guidelines for permanence and durability
of the Committee on Production Guidelines for Book Longevity
of the Council of Library Resources.

© 2008 Peter Lang Publishing, Inc., New York
29 Broadway, 18th floor, New York, NY 10006
www.peterlang.com

Printed in the United States of America

We dedicate this volume to two very special people whose passing during the process of writing this book gave us great pause in how we understand the need for human connectedness in our everyday lives. To them we owe our gratitude for teaching us how to turn toward the other in authentic and practical ways.

To my father-in-law, Elmer "Bud" Cook, a true gentleman and family man. I know he was proud of my accomplishments, and he entered heaven the day before I saw him to tell him about this book being accepted for publication. Now he knows, and he has my love always.

—Melissa

To my mom, Elizabeth June Umberger. Your passing marked my life in an unprecedented way but you will always be with me in my thoughts, my heart, and my volition.

—Annette

Contents

Foreword

Michael J. Hyde

Present-day teaching and research in the related areas of philosophy of communication and communicative ethics speak ancient wisdom about the art of rhetoric. Such wisdom is found, for example, in the writings of Cicero. Commenting on the cultural and educational influence exerted by Socrates' and Plato's critical assessment of the orator's art, Cicero accused the assessment of bringing about "the undoubtedly absurd and unprofitable and reprehensible severance between the tongue and the brain, leading to our having one set of professors to teach us to think and another to teach us to speak" (*De Oratore*, 3.16.61). This accusation was not intended as a mere put-down of philosophy. Like Socrates, Plato, and Aristotle before him, Cicero held firmly to the belief that if we bestow fluency of speech on persons devoid of the virtues of integrity and supreme wisdom, we shall not have made ethically minded orators of them but shall have put weapons into the hands of madmen. Cicero also insisted, however, that we are not born for ourselves alone, that our country claims a share of our being, and that if we intend to contribute to the general good, we must not disparage and retreat from the politics of public life, but instead use our skill, industry, and talents to bond human society more closely together. The severance between the tongue and the brain is an impediment to this civic-minded, persuasive, and moral endeavor. Philosophy and the rhetorical and ethical workings of communication must walk hand in hand for the betterment of humankind.

The present volume of original chapters, arranged and edited by Professors Melissa Cook and Annette Holba, is dedicated to encourage and further inform intellectually and practically this engagement of disciplines. Contributors draw theoretical direction from influential philosophers such as Mikhail Bakhtin, Martin Buber, Hans-Georg Gadamer, Jürgen Habermas, Alasdair MacIntyre, Paul Ricoeur, and Calvin Schrag. Case studies—emphasizing topics such as intercultural communication, narrative ethics and the feminist voice, public relation practices, communication in the pedagogical setting, and the enactment of rhetorical consciousness in organizations—provide concrete, praxis-oriented illustrations of what these and a host of other thinkers have to say about the scope and function of communication ethics. Hence, the authors promote the argument with these case studies that the value of any philosophy of communication resides in the practical insights it provides into ongoing ethical and moral problems.

The legitimacy of this argument has a long history, and its future is guaranteed as long as we continue to be challenged by the openness, uncertainty, and contingency of our future-oriented existence. The challenge sounds a call of conscience that confronts us with the fundamental responsibility of finding ways to make known the useful and the inexpedient, the fitting and the improper, and the just and the unjust as we engage others in collaborative deliberation about contestable matters. The chapters offered by Professors Cook, Holba, and their colleagues warrant praise for how they alert and help us to understand the importance of this process of communication ethics.

Acknowledgments

We thank all of the contributors to this edited volume for their work and dedication to complete an inspiring discussion on how we can move philosophy of communication into everyday experiences. We especially thank our colleagues who offered their scholarship for this volume including, Rev. John Amankwah, S. Alyssa Groom, Fadoua Loudiy, Marie Baker Ohler, John H. Prellwitz, and Elesha L. Ruminski. Their work here represents the *walking of the humanities into the marketplace* and we thank them for their dedication to this project. We appreciate the opening remarks from Michael J. Hyde and the conclusion from Ronald C. Arnett, our esteemed colleagues who light our paths.

We recognize and appreciate the encouragement we continually receive from Pat Arneson, Ronald C. Arnett, Cynthia Burke, Janie M. Harden Fritz, Kathleen Glenister Roberts, Richard H. Thames, and Calvin L. Troup. We also appreciate the support received from our peers–the faculty and administration at St. Vincent College and Plymouth State University.

We have been blessed by having students who are eager to explore philosophy of communication and we thank them for their participation in our discussions. The students of St. Vincent College and Plymouth State University are eager and energetic, and we thank them for their contributions to our work. Melissa Kaminski at St. Vincent College was a valuable research and copywriting assistant to Melissa Cook and we thank her for her time, attention to detail, and enthusiasm.

Much appreciation and thanks to the associates at Peter Lang Publishing who assisted us in the production and publication of our work. We appreciate their professionalism throughout this process.

Finally, we thank our families and friends for their encouragement of our work. The Webber, Cook, Allwein, Umberger, and Holba families have our respect, love, and appreciation for giving us our space and support when we needed it most. Melissa extends her deepest love to David, Catherine, and David, Jr. Annette extends her deepest love to Dan, their children and Springer Spaniel, Emily.

Introduction

Our purpose in editing this book that integrates philosophies of communication and communication ethics is threefold. First, we want to provide multiple perspectives on practical application of philosophies of communication and communication ethics. This means we want to invite the upper-level undergraduate and graduate student to see how dense concepts involving philosophies and ethics can help to inform and guide communicative exchanges. So, we invited authors to contribute their work that is theoretically sophisticated yet grounded in the real world. Second, we offer perspectives that come from a postmodern engagement of philosophies of communication and communication ethics, which recognize new ways to communicate that open dialogue, embrace diversity, and acknowledge the need for grounded philosophical and practical discourse. Third, we also wanted to celebrate new scholarly voices focusing on praxial aspects of human communication.

The invited scholars come from a particular tradition of rhetorical studies that privileges philosophies of communication and communication ethics as an interpretive approach to the study of communication. The authors have a common ground that is distinctly different from quantitative, qualitative, and critical approaches to communication scholarship. Each author engages research from a constructive hermeneutic approach that is designed to cultivate the serendipitous in research approaches. Because of this collective hermeneutical perspective we invited scholars Michael J. Hyde and Ronald C. Arnett to write a foreword and conclusion, respectively, as both of their work has contributed to the scholarly development of each author.

The approach to the application of philosophies of communication and communication ethics is unique to the field as this book seeks to integrate both philosophies of communication and communication ethics in one project that demonstrates the overlap and synthesis of their interplay in our everyday communicative practices. We begin this introduction with defining how we use philosophies of communication and communication ethics, both of which are important considerations in our postmodern era, where narrative contention and uncertainty of the unknown and the known prevail.

Philosophy of Communication

To define philosophy of communication we first begin by defining the terms of the couplet individually that permits our understanding of communication to emerge unhampered by assumption or ambiguity. In asking what is philosophy, some basic definitions will suffice, after which more in-depth definitions can be developed. According to the _Cambridge Dictionary of Philosophy, philosophia perennis_ is "a supposed body of truths that appear in the writings of the great philosophers, or the truths common to opposed philosophical viewpoints" (Audi, 1999, p. 667) All disciplines have a philosophy or philosophies in which there is a particular body of truths or in which there is a particular search for truths. This means a worldview is explored within all disciplines. This is a search for a truth, but that truth may be different from another truth.

Other definitions of philosophy include what points of view are all about or an "overview that usually embraces both value-commitments and beliefs about the general nature of things" (Flew, 1979, p. vii). Another question that might be helpful is, "What is it that distinguishes this _as_ philosophical?" It could refer to "an examination of the presuppositions and implications of scientific practice [...that] reveal[s] the authentic objective knowledge" (Flew, 1979, p. ix). Philosophy is of itself and yet of other articles too. One may call these _branches_, such as, aesthetics, ethics, epistemology, logic, and metaphysics. All these articles can be used to explore disciplines such as philosophy of mathematics, law, science, psychology, communication, and many others. There are political philosophies, social philosophies, cultural philosophies, and so on. Therefore, a philosophy is part, it is also whole, and it can be pursued through different lenses.

Greek philosophy means _love of knowledge_ or _wisdom_. It is the "study of the most general and abstract features of the world and categories with which we think: mind, matter, reason, proof, truth" (Blackburn, 1996, p. 286). Philosophy of a particular discipline studies "the concepts that structure such thinking, and to lay bare their foundations and presuppositions" (Blackburn, 1996, p. 286). This means that philosophy is not pursued to solve problems of the law, science, or anything of an empirical nature. Philosophy is to seek a truth for the purpose of itself, to _find out_ rather than to _fix_.

From the Latin, _philosophia, -ae, f_ means theory or _ration, -onis_ (Traupman, 1994, p. 592). This theory or rationale, inherent to this

Latin reference, implies the Romans worked with presuppositions too. The Romans borrowed the Greek ideas of reason, proof, truths, and worked within their own particular framework of presuppositions.

So, philosophy can be shaped in a particular fashion but at its essence *philosophy is a mode of thinking about something.* The thinking is shaped from presuppositions and generally taken as a worldview. The something that is thought about is not as important as the way of thinking, through structure, foundation, and asking the question "What *is* this about?" Philosophy has developed into many schools of thought. Often overlapping others or evolving and diverging from others. Philosophy is the thinking about things because of a love of wisdom, a love of knowledge, and a desire to find the truth—then it could be enough, *satis.* Or could it? This notion of *satis* can never be found because questions never end, so philosophy is infinite—it must be.

Moving on to the term "communication" and starting with the *Cambridge Dictionary of Philosophy,* communication is referred to as information theory or communication theory. It is a mathematical theory of communication. Its "objective feature of information explains its potential for epistemic and semantic development by philosophers" (Audi, 1999, p. 435). This, however, is not broad enough; rather it is couched within a specific area of communication. Perhaps a better definition may be the transmission of information (Blackburn, 1996). One communication theory textbook defines communication as being hard to define because scholars "hold widely divergent views as to what communication is" (Griffin, 2000, p. 34). Rather, a collective look at communication through the differing theories can produce a broad definition. Communication can be anatomized as interpersonal influence, information processing, public address, sharing meanings through signs, creation and enactment of a social reality, reflective challenges of unjust discourse, and dialogue. It seems that communication is the way beings communicate—or transfer meanings to one another.

A multidisciplinary definition of communication could consider communication as an umbrella term for many concepts. Most communication concepts involve organized sets of variables that are interrelated in complex ways and work within particular contexts. Philosophically, for Martin Buber (1955), communication occurs through dialogue and this dialogue can be silent although still be-

ing considered speech. This is his notion of the I-Thou, a communication or dialogue that occurs in the *between*. In *Dialogic Civility in
a Cynical Age*, Ronald C. Arnett and Pat Arneson (1999) argue that
"[d]ialogue brings us face to face with life as it is, not as we hope it
would be" (p. 144). They suggest Buber's "philosophy of communication is not to be confused with a communicative system of comfort
or a set of blinders permitting one to ignore the pain of the human
struggle" (p. 144). It seems here that not only is communication
spoken and not spoken but also it is intended to bring participants
closer to a truth rather than be a barrier to it.

Pragmatically, for Marcus Cicero (2000), communication occurs
through rhetoric. One must communicate to get one's point across,
whether through forensic, deliberative, or epideictic oratory, so that
the rhetor can persuade another to a particular viewpoint. In other
words, an act of speech can be "a unit of communication having evaluative and judgmental aspects as well as acoustical, physiological,
and linguistic dimensions" (Wallace, 1970, p. 174).

Communication can be "the transmission or exchange of information [...] and the science and practice of transmitting information" and it is an "access or means of access between persons or
places [...] a connecting door [or] passage" (Brown, 1993, p. 455).
This sharing or transmitting of information can be in the public
and private, such as, interpersonal situations, groups, in business,
and government. Communication is how beings *mean* to each other.
Communication is not limited to language, as it takes any shape or
form and it results with the passing along of a meaning. This overview leads us to one of the most important questions relevant to our
book, "What is Philosophy of Communication?" The natural answer
to this question would be to say that it is the intersection of the two
disciplines, philosophy and communication—and it is much more
than that as well. If you take the realms where human communication and philosophy meet there is significant overlap. First, in communication one can study interpersonal, intercultural, marketing,
advertising, public relations, and so on. Then philosophers, people
pursuing questions of method, effectiveness, realities, multiplicities,
trying to understand the why, how, and what for questions, will approach these questions through epistemology, ethics, history, and a
historical ground. This is where the two concepts of philosophy and
communication will meet and continue the pursuit of their inquiry.

An example of the intersection of philosophy and communication is Jürgen Habermas' (1984) *Theory of Communicative Action* in which the author deals with three perspectives. First, he opens the concept of rationality of modern philosophy and social theory. Next, he constructs a bi-level concept of society that integrates what he describes as the lifeworld and system paradigm. Finally, he sketches out a theory of modernity that explores and considers its own pathologies. Habermas believes that to have an adequate theory of society one must integrate methods that can help to negate previously created polarization. Habermas already sees the need for overlap between disciplines. He suggests a communicative action that recognizes this overlap, as he argues,

> If we assume that the human species maintains itself through socially coordinated activities of its members and that this coordination is established through communication—and in certain spheres of life, through communication aimed at reaching agreement—then the reproduction of the species *also* requires satisfying the conditions of a rationality inherent in communicative action. (1984, p. 397)

Habermas is saying that language, in communication, needs to be seen not as grammar but as dialectic, with a rationality that is inherent in the very nature of the communicative act. This rationality must be found within the overlap of philosophy and communication.

In Habermas's (1987) notion of the lifeworld intersection with the systems paradigm, he suggests that

> [e]veryday communicative practice is [...] embedded in a lifeworld context defined by cultural tradition, legitimate orders, and socialized individuals. Interpretive performances draw upon and advance consensus. The rationality potential of mutual understanding in language is actualized to the extent that motive and value generalization progress and the zones of what is unproblematic shrink. (p. 183)

Communication occurs within tradition, a rationality of existence, a particular social order, between the individual and the community. Therefore, in understanding or recognizing the rationale of such communication, working from Habermas's lifeworld paradigm, not remaining alone in a systems only paradigm, problems of understanding can be reduced. In this way, recognizing and working within the overlap of communication and philosophy can be effective and contribute constructively to understanding how human beings *mean*.

Other philosophers work from other perspectives with emphases on their interest area. For example, Hans-Georg Gadamer examines methods of communication and explores the how and what for questions. His inquiry leads to particular action and direction for which he advocates. Most important for Gadamer is to look at communication through a philosophical hermeneutic. He engages, philosophically, how we understand. His work, *Philosophical Hermeneutics* (Gadamer, 1977), begins with the question "Why has the problem of language come to occupy the same central position in current philosophical discussions that the concept of thought, or 'thought thinking of itself,' held in philosophy a century a half ago?" (p. 3). This question opens his discussion of philosophical hermeneutics, and he directly links to this language as "the fundamental mode of operation of our being-in-the-world" (p. 3). So, this venture into his discussion of philosophical hermeneutics begins with the essential way man/woman communicates, through language. Gadamer's philosophy is this intersection between philosophy and communication. This assertion is addressed by Stanley Deetz (1978), who argues that "hermeneutics relates to current problems with communication research and the dominant current conception of human understanding" (p. 12). In other words, according to Deetz there are limits to traditional communication research and that using Gadamer's hermeneutics to frame or reconstruct communication studies, will "give a sense of perspective [...] and a legitimate mode of thinking and working" (p. 12). Deetz also argues that most communication researchers do not understand hermeneutics or use a hermeneutic lens through which to view research, which is why he calls for a better understanding of communication through a hermeneutic rather than a strict stance based on quantitative and qualitative processes.

Scholars who work within this intersection of philosophy and communication point toward a reflection of how people have communicated through history with each other. These reflections are essential to the examination or contemplation of where the human condition (existence) has been and is moving toward. Modern scholar Hannah Arendt (1998) argued that the problem of the human condition is that communication has fallen into the realm of a *social*, leaving the dimensions of the public and private, essential to humankind, in a state of confusion. Arendt argued that the distinction between the public and private realm should equal "the distinction between things that should be shown and things that should be hidden" (p. 72). She argued that this private realm has withered away into a blurred reality where that distinction no longer exists. Arendt's contribution to philosophy of communication engages a conversation about the state of humankind. As we employ the couplet communication ethics in this work we must also ask our readers to think not of "a" philosophy of communication but to embrace the consideration of "philosophies of communication" in that same vein. To assume one philosophy of something negates our purpose, which is to take a journey though the multiplicity of philosophies that one might encounter in the everyday act of communicating with others. As mentioned earlier, philosophies of communication is only one aspect of this work. Communication ethics is the other beacon that guides this project, and we now consider the question, what is communication ethics?

Communication Ethics

Over the past 60 years, scholars have engaged in the differentiation of communication ethics from ethics. Richard L. Johannesen (2002) wrote an extensive and incredibly useful compilation work on communication ethics in his highly revered text on *Ethics in Human Communication*. In this text, Johannesen investigates human communication and ethics to provide a categorical outline and discussion of communication ethics from various perspectives as well as presenting case studies at the end of the fifth edition. Johannesen (2002) explains his main contention in relating communication and ethics by suggesting that

> [p]otential ethical issues are inherent in any instance of communication between humans to the degree that the communication can be judged on a right-wrong dimension, that it involves possible significance on humans, and that the communicator consciously chooses specific ends sought and communicative means to achieve those ends. (p. 2)

Communication ethics involves choices, duty, obligation, right and wrong, and how one makes a decision and then articulates it to another.

On a microlevel, these are significant components found within interpersonal relationships that must be identified and understood to effect relationships in a constructive way. On a macrolevel, decision making affects societies in total. Therefore, communication ethics needs to move from a theoretical discussion to a practical application for dialogue and language to be used in communication.

Since "[L]anguage is a tool that can be used in better or worse ways to achieve human goals," Sharon L. Bracci and Clifford G. Christians (2002) see communication ethicists and moral theorists working in tandem, both groups considering methods to "evaluate the use of language" to explain *why to evaluate* means used to achieve certain ends (p. 1). "While moral philosophers speculate broadly about the nature and grounds of being a good person, communication ethicists focus on the ethical person in and through language" (Bracci & Christians, 2002, p. 2). Our field has continued to expand, as Ronald C. Arnett (1991) outlined in his review of communication ethics scholarship in communication journals over a 50-year period of the twentieth century.

In Ronald C. Arnett's (1991) description and analysis of the scholarly works in the field of communication ethics, he explained that the main perspective outlined by theorists and contributors to communication ethics texts is "choice making" (p. 56). When we make an ethical decision, the fact that we *have a choice to make* is what turns us from the theoretical to the practical. Aristotle explained his use of the word *phronesis*, as Arnett outlined, the "focus on deliberative choice via practical discourse [can be] found in Aristotle's *Nicomachean ethics*" (Arnett, 1991, p. 56). Aristotle's work points toward communication ethics as forms of *phronesis* and decision making.

Similar to Ronald C. Arnett's article on the status of communication ethics scholarship, Richard L. Johannesen (2001) wrote of the trends in the field of communication ethics as well as pointed toward what those trends recommend for future research agendas in his article "Communication Ethics: Centrality, Trends, and Controversies" (pp. 201–235). Johannesen explained that when viewing the self, it should not be as an emotivistic, modern self, but rather as a "situated, embedded, socially constructed self," perhaps located within an organization (p. 227). This article is an excellent bibliographic source, as Johannesen offers detailed analysis of the writings on communication ethics in the past two decades and suggests trends that include media, organizational, individual and social ethics, freedom and responsibility, ethic of care, and virtue or character ethics.

As Johannesen (2002) consistently explains in his analysis of the literature on communication ethics, consideration needs to be given to communication ethics in a postmodern world. This can be a challenge, but a welcome challenge, as diversity, culture, and technology all influence how we act and react within our separate, yet technologically related cultures. Situating communication ethics within the real world is a necessity that scholars realize in writing about the need for a *praxis* orientation.

Communication ethics is ethics in action. A crucial component of communication ethics is investigating how society communicates and the methods and media used. Communication ethics scholar Kenneth E. Anderson (1991) considers the need to look at how history and the medium (technology) used for communication affected the practices and the communicative theories of the day. For example, Greek communication was oral, the printing press enacted the shift during the Enlightenment to written, and now, cyber/computer mediated-technology has affected modernity (Anderson, 1991, pp. 4–5). Throughout this work, various types of "media" will be reviewed, from basic narrative, to poetry, to fictitious novels, to historical biographies, so that an interpretive narrative can be used to bring forth the communication ethic of the various time periods discussed.

Pat Arneson (2007) reminds us that a history of communication ethics has not been fully written yet but communication ethics scholars are now working toward providing a historical backdrop that will undergird our understanding of communication ethics. What we do know is that ethics are an indispensable part of human communication (Arneson, 2007). In addition, ethics in human communication deal with questions of "how one should live one's life" (Arneson, 2007, p. xiii). Arneson identifies eight fundamental "*domains*" (p. xiii) for the consideration and application of communication ethics that include interpersonal communication; small group communication; organizational communication; rhetorical communication; advertising, public relations, and marketing; and news media. She reminds us (1) of the multiplicity and complexity of the engagement of critical thinking in these domains; (2) that rights and responsibilities go hand in hand when asserting one's communicative freedom; and (3) to study communication ethics we need to study ideas that are "continually augmented by what one learns" from others (p. xviii). We respond to Arneson's call for mindfulness to the study of communication ethics by including the multiple perspectives and domains of inquiry that follow in the subsequent chapters of this book.

Ethics will continue to be discussed as society changes. There is no right or wrong answer when deciding on ethical decisions and outcomes, as "ethical considerations form an integral part of human existence and are constantly disputed. Human beings argue about ethics partly because it is so central to their lives" (Machan, 1997, p. 5). As those within society are in constant dialogue with each other, those involved in the dialogue will be questioned as well as perform the questioning as to what ought to be done. Every corner turned, whether done consciously or not, one can ask questions that have ethical communicative considerations on a daily basis. In today's postmodern culture, differences need to be recognized with society inviting dialogue, not just with people, but also with changing historical conditions (Makau & Arnett, 1997, p. x). We now move to describe the chapters that follow in our discovery of the place of philosophies of communication and communication ethics in human communication.

Description

This book is an upper-level undergraduate/graduate reader for courses including Interpersonal Communication, Organizational Communication, Communication Ethics, or Philosophy of Communication. This reader can be used independently from other textbooks or it complements a standard textbook, and it provides students with the opportunity to consider multiple ways of enhancing human communication through discovering how philosophies of communication and communication ethics shape and guide communicative exchanges. Each chapter is philosophical and pragmatic with questions addressing issues of either philosophies of communication and/or communication ethics in interpersonal and organizational communicative contexts that involve intercultural, marketplace, political, and feminist perspectives. Communication in organizations comes in many forms and contexts. Interpersonal communication is an integral part of communication in the marketplace as people move between public and private sphere engagement. Whether communicating in the public realm as part of a small group or organization, or in the private realm as part of an interpersonal dyad, one develops competencies situated within and "between" philosophies of communication and communication ethics. This reader is designed to enhance an active learning environment by cultivating classroom discussion, engagement, and the understanding/comprehension of deeply theoretical issues in real life contexts. This text provides students the opportunity to develop or improve critical thinking skills that help them negotiate questions of philosophies and ethics in their everyday communicative encounters.

We explore the following themes and metaphors: *schadenfreude*, communicative political advocacy, communication in the pedagogical setting, narrative hermeneutics, and a case study of identity and memory in Morocco, ethical public relations practices, narrative literacy and the feminist voice, ethics of care, and the rhetorical consciousness in marketing within interpersonal and/or organizational contexts. Each chapter deals with issues that students may encounter on a day-to-day basis and offers alternative ways to approach communicative encounters more efficiently, effectively, and responsibly.

Summary of Chapters

In Chapter 1, "Understanding *Schadenfreude* to Seek an Ethical Response," the author considers the emergence of *shadenfreude*, experiencing joy from one's contribution to the loss/failure/demise of others, in a postmodern world where human communication vacillates between cosmopolitan and provincial environments. This is a uniquely American understanding of *schadenfreude* that is distinctly different from its original birth in the German language that does not focus on negative intentions or effects of the action itself. The emergence of *schadenfreude* and its potential consequences in human relationships invites philosophical and ethical questions regarding marketplace and interpersonal communicative practices. To connect to the real world, a hypothetical example asks one to rethink the nature of *schadenfreude* in the workplace—how we deal with it as opposed to how we ought to deal with it.

In Chapter 2, "Political Communication and Ethical 'Celebrity Advocacy,'" the author considers different philosophical perspectives on communication ethics that may constructively address choices confronting organizations at the macro level as well as decision making at the personal level, inside and outside specific organizations. This chapter explores the effects of ethical advocacy on decision making in the private and public political processes. Analyzing competing narratives and decision making through a variety of philosophical and ethical paradigms permits fruitful discussion of whether such public communication (advocacy) weakens or

strengthens debate within a democracy charged with crucial decision-making duties and offers pragmatic choices for the process of
public advocacy.

In Chapter 3, "Ethical Dialogue in the Classroom," the author points toward cultivating a new understanding of a classroom
environment that hinges on ethical dialogue that broadens the
classroom conversation. A new form of dialogic interaction in the
classroom is necessary to enhance and facilitate the student-teacher
learning process and to form a community of hope that grapples
with emerging difficulties and demands of everyday life.

In Chapter 4, "Narrative Identity and Public Memory in Morocco," the author explains that vernacular narratives can offer those in
the present a way to deal with atrocities of the past in a proper manner allowing for recognition of the problems and an ethical outlet for
current situations. People often talk about learning from their past,
and this chapter gives an excellent case study based on current issues in Morocco. Public memory is offered as a vehicle for self-understanding and ethical responses to rhetorical interruptions.

In Chapter 5, "Dialogic Meeting: A Constructive Rhetorical Approach to Contemporary Public Relations Practice," the author engages narrative contention in the postmodern marketplace through
the lens of Mikhail Bakhtin's dialogic grounding of rhetoric and offers the metaphor of *dialogic meeting* as an ethically grounded guide
for the public relations practitioner. In a postmodern marketplace
where narrative contention is commonplace in public discourse, the
contemporary practice of public relations calls for pragmatic attention to ethically driven practices. Practicing public relations through
the perspective of dialogic meeting mutually reinforces the intersection of word and deed that is necessary to negotiate in a postmodern
marketplace.

In Chapter 6, "Narrative Literacy: A Communicative Practice of
Interpretation for the Ethical Deliberation of Contentious Organizational Narratives," narrative literacy is explored through a conscious reading of narratives framed by an ethic through the metaphor of dialogic civility. Narrative literacy can assist us in tolerating
increased ambiguity in various interpersonal and organizational
contexts, a requirement for communicating ethically in a postmodern time. The idea that narrative literacy can also enhance the invitation and reception of women's voices within narrative contexts is
also explored in an applied context.

Chapter 7, "Dialogue as the Labor of Care: The Necessity of a Unity of Contraries within Interpersonal Communication," brings together the various philosophies of caring from the disciplines of psychology, nursing, philosophy, feminist theory, and communication. Through an interdisciplinary approach, this chapter considers ideas on caring under the assertion that caring is communicatively constituted. In doing so, the meeting "between" the philosophy of caring and its application for everyday communicative life plays out in five distinct metaphors: obligation, relation, the particular other, the ability to care and be cared for, and finally, the horizon of significant outcomes. To illuminate the applicability of this communicative ethic, the metaphors are seen through the lens of the literary work of Victor Hugo, specifically *Les Miserables*.

In Chapter 8, "Engaging the Rhetorical Consciousness of an Organization for Dynamic Communicative Exchange," the author discusses the nature and development of a relationship between an organization and its internal and external constituents that is increasingly the focus when developing a framework for public, organizational communication. In a historical moment shaped by an accelerated rate of technological change, intracultural lifestyles, and a heightened commoditization of personal preference, the importance of organizational communication as more than a means to profitability has grown exponentially. The rhetorical consciousness of an organization—a praxis mode of communicative interaction for the purposes of ethical engagement—is posited as a philosophical and practical point of departure for a communicative framework of an organization. The intent of the chapter is to identify foundational coordinates for engaging organizational communication as a storied phenomenon.

References

Anderson, Kenneth E. (1991). A history of communication ethics. In K. Joy (Ed.), *Conversations on communication ethics* (pp. 3–20). Norwood, NJ: Ablex.

Arendt, H. (1998). *The human condition*. Chicago: University of Chicago.

Arneson, P. (2007). *Exploring communication ethics: Interviews with influential scholars in the field*. New York: Peter Lang.

Arnett, R.C. (1991). The status of communication ethics scholarship in speech communication journals from 1915 to 1985. In K. Joy (Ed.), *Conversations on communication ethics* (pp. 55–72). Norwood, NJ: Ablex.

Arnett, R. C., & Arneson, P. (1999). *Dialogic civility in a cynical age: Community, hope, and interpersonal relationships*. Albany: State University of New York Press.

Audi, R. (1999). *The Cambridge dictionary of philosophy.* Cambridge: Cambridge University Press.

Blackburn, S. (1996). *The Oxford dictionary of philosophy.* New York: Oxford University Press.

Bracci, S. L., & Christians, C. G. (2002). Introduction. In S. L. Bracci & C. G. Christians (Eds.), *Moral engagement in public life: Theorists for contemporary ethics* (pp. 1–15). New York: Peter Lang.

Brown, L. (1993). *The new shorter Oxford English dictionary.* (Thumb Index Edition). New York: Oxford University Press.

Buber, M. (1955). *Between man and man.* Boston: Beacon Press.

Cicero, M. (2000). *De inventione, de optimo genere oratorum, topica.* Cambridge, MA: Harvard University Press.

Deetz, S. (1978). Conceptualizing human understanding: Gadamer's hermeneutics and American communication studies. *Communication Quarterly, 26* (2), 12–23.

Flew, A. (1979). *A dictionary of philosophy.* New York: Gramercy Books.

Gadamer, H. G. (1977). *Philosophical hermeneutics.* Berkeley: University of California Press.

Griffin, E. (2000). *A first look at communication theory.* Boston: McGraw Hill.

Habermas, J. (1984). *The theory of communicative action: Reason and the rationalization of society* (Vol. 1). Boston: Beacon Press.

Habermas, J. (1987). *The theory of communicative action: Lifeworld and system: A critique of functionalist reason* (Vol. 2). Boston: Beacon Press.

Johannesen, R. L. (2001). Communication ethics: Centrality, trends, and controversies. *Communication Yearbook, 25,* 201–235.

———. (2002). *Ethics in human communication.* Long Grove, IL: Waveland Press.

Machan, T. R. (1997). *A primer on ethics.* Norman: University of Oklahoma Press.

Makau, J., & Arnett, R. C. (1997). Preface. In J. Makau & R. C. Arnett (Eds.), *Communication ethics in an age of diversity* (pp. vii–xi). Chicago: University of Illinois Press.

Traupman, J. (1994). *The new college Latin & English dictionary.* New York: Bantam.

Wallace, K. R. (1970). Speech act unit of communication. *Philosophy and Rhetoric, 3,* 174–181.

Chapter 1

Understanding *Schadenfreude* to Seek an Ethical Response

Annette M. Holba

> You can kill a man but you can't kill what he stands for, So, you kill his spirit...that's a beautiful thing to see. —*X-Files*, Fox TV, May 25, 2006

Americans and Germans have different understandings of the term *schadenfreude* (Portmann, 2000). An American understanding of the term is very limited and focused compared with the German understanding that is very broad and complex. In the United States we see *schadenfreude* mediated to us through the tabloids and sophisticated news reports, yet we do not identify it for what it really is. In a postmodern world when *schadenfreude* pervades multiple venues, we can no longer ignore its existence or the need to respond to it. How we respond to *schadenfreude* can shape the human experience that follows. A postmodern world invites us to respond to such an affront because our lives are no longer limited within a provincial environment as we hear a more cosmopolitan narrative call for communicative engagement with others. Since *schadenfreude* is intertwined in our everyday lives, we must find an ethical response that is appropriate in our postmodern world.

This chapter first defines *schadenfreude* from both German and American cultural perspectives. Aspects of *schadenfreude* are discussed through dualistic metaphors of civility/incivility, agency/embeddedness, and trust/skepticism. Second, this chapter discusses ethical considerations related to acts of *schadenfreude* in our world today. Third, Eric Dezenhall's call to enact dissuasion as an ethical response of dialectical advocacy to the practice of *schadenfreude* is advanced. Next, a real world exemplar of responding to *schadenfreude* is offered, and finally, this chapter discusses implications for further scholarly study of *schadenfreude* from a communication perspective. *Schadenfreude* is an experience that we have all encountered in some form or another.

What Is *Schadenfreude*?

Eric Dezenhall (1999) argues that we are living in a "culture of attack" (p. 117). In a culture of attack, mindless attacks on high-profile people are precipitated by one of the seven deadly sins, invidia, envy, or in a vernacular sense, jealousy. These attacks are not to reveal bad actions but rather to bring another person to his or her public or private disgrace and/or demise. In these attacks we find malice, falsehoods, distortions, and hidden agendas of the attackers (Dezenhall, 1999). Dezenhall points to some of the more recognizable acts of *schadenfreude*, such as the media attacks on TV personality Kathie Lee Gifford and sweatshops, former Speaker of the House Newt Gingrich's swift attack on reporter Connie Chung after her nationally viewed interview with his mother, former Special Prosecutor Ken Starr's obsessive attack on President Bill Clinton, and pop singer Michael Jackson's repetitive struggle with accusations of child sexual abuse. Although these are examples involving famous people, acts of *schadenfreude* occur in every human circle, rich or poor, strong or weak.

An American understanding of *schadenfreude* presupposes that it is okay to attack individuals or entities that are different, successful, or "outside" one's concept of normalcy. It can also be suggested that acts of *schadenfreude* happen when one person is jealous of another person's success or "perceived" success. According to American conceptualization, *schadenfreude* means to take pleasure in the misfortunes of others (Anonymous, 2003; Peverley, 2005; Zagorin, 2000), feeling a malicious pleasure at the fall of another's fortunes (Leach, Spears, Branscombe & Doosje, 2003), and feeling the "ecstasy of defeat" of another (Rushin, 2002, p. 23). This is owing to one's desire to see another lose what she or he has earned. Typically, this attitude is propelled by lust, envy, hatred, jealousy, or the need to gain attention for one's self. Dezenhall (1999) suggests that these attacks require six elements:

Victim—someone who claims to have suffered injustice.

Villain—target of attack.

Vindicator—the redeemer sent to right the wrong at any cost.

Void—unfulfilled public need causing others to tune into the story.

Vehicle—the medium that delivers the attack.

Value—the social principle under which the attack is delivered/made. (p. 13)

The O. J. Simpson murder case is used as an example because it can be assumed that most people are aware of the case, and therefore, there is no need to state the case in point. Dezenhall (1999) suggests that O. J. Simpson can be considered a victim in the case being pursued by a villain, Mark Furman, the investigating detective. The vindicator would be considered the press or the defense council of O. J. Simpson. This is the entity that tries to right the wrong. The void in this case, that unfulfilled need that fuels the public desire to stay focused on the story, is race redemption. The issue here is that a black man was charged with the murder of two white people. Historically, black Americans have been at a disadvantage in the court system for economic and other reasons. The public stayed in tune with the story, as the story would be affected by race relations and race redemption issues. The vehicle in this case is the press, television, newspaper, and movies. Any form of mass media was helpful in delivering the attack against Furman, who became the focus of the case, not the actual deaths of two people. Finally, the value or social principle that underlies the attack itself is delivered. In this case, the idea of racial equality (for all the injustice in the past) would take precedence over physical evidence and actual truth in the case.

Examining public situations or situations in your personal life can yield better understanding of how we come to encounter acts of *schadenfreude*. Dezenhall asks how we came to this place in our human condition. He suggests these causation patterns as part of the conditioning that creates *schadenfreude*:

Discontent—the engine that drives the culture of *schadenfreude*.

News Media—rewards absolute conclusions—this is the vehicle that transports the culture of *schadenfreude*.

Declining Standards of Decorum—in general we have declining standards and the lack of restraint in decorum has allowed or created the opportunity for people to become mean toward one another.

Dezenhall is crafting a narrowly focused American understanding of *schadenfreude*. This understanding of *schadenfreude* is
distinctly American because most of the written literature, scholarly
or trade, depicts *schadenfreude* in this way—very one-dimensional.
However, there is another dimension to *schadenfreude* that is often
overlooked in American culture. Immanuel Kant (1956) believed
that certain people deserved to suffer because of their own actions.
However, Kant distinguishes between the approving of suffering
and the celebration of suffering.

Schadenfreude has its origin in the German language, *schaden*
meaning damage and *freude* meaning joy. Together we understand
this to mean one's joy or pleasure for another's damage or demise.
If some people can't achieve the American Dream as they watch
others achieve it, "they make damn sure that somebody else can't
either" (Dezenhall, 1999, p. 116). This is embodied *schadenfreude*
at work. The goal of one's actions is to knock the other down (often
below the belt). In *schadenfreude*, one's phenomenological focus of
attention is toward the other driven by agency toward a negative
outcome. Typically, acts of *schadenfreude* neglect ethical introspec-
tion and seek to uplift the self by contributing to or causing the
downfall of another.

Other linguistic dimensions of the term *schadenfreude* include
"malice," "cruelty," and "misery" (Portmann, 2000, p. 3). Other
translation includes being connected to a "deservedness" of suffering
(Portmann, 2000, p. 4). These connotations have become
representative of the American conceptualization of *schadenfreude*. In instances when *schadenfreude* is morally acceptable, it
signifies a "love of justice" that begins the distinction between
American and German grappling of the term itself (Portmann,
2000, p. 4). There is certainly no word or concept
that is parallel in the English language. In the German "*Bösheit
und Schadenfreude*," the *und* means to make a distinction between
the two terms *Bösheit* and *Schadenfreude*. Portmann (2000) considers *schadenfreude* to be a potential subset of malice.

In Kafka's (1992) discussion on the conscious, he asserts five
contingent and ambiguous presuppositions pertaining to malice:
(1) it is a synonym for *schadenfreude*, (2) *schadenfreude* presupposes
malice, (3) there is a social importance of what others think we de-
serve, (4) there is a moral import connected to *schadenfreude*, and
(5) cruelty is part of *schadenfreude*. Portmann (2000) translated

Kafka's text in which he finds these ambivalent tensions at play in consideration of *schadenfreude*. These considerations of malice and *schadenfreude* demonstrate the complexities inherent in describing *schadenfreude* in a one-dimensioal manner. Part of this lingual ambivalence and the multiple perspectives on *schadenfreude* is determined by the idea that there is no equivalent in the English language. Therefore, as the term is translated, the bias or preference of the translated emerges and helps to frame or shape a conceptual understanding.

There is a difference between thinking someone deserves suffering and causing that suffering. Our understanding of *schadenfreude* teeters sometimes ambiguously between these two ends or extremes. Conceptualization is also confounded in the notion of *schadenfreude* because it pits people against one another (Portmann, 2000). Portmann argues that no matter what, "*schadenfreude* will persist because of differing moral beliefs" (p. 15) of *schadenfreude* at play because of human tendency to competition, social comparison, emotivism, and the darker side that includes,malice, cruelty, sadism, and envy.

Portmann (2000) disagrees with the American conceptualization of *schadenfreude*, as he argues that "*schadenfreude* should not be considered malicious pleasure for the reason that it usually does not involve expectation, much less agency" (p. 22). However, this broad statement is open to contention. Much of the *schadenfreude*, at least what is seen in American culture, involves an expectation, an act of one's will, an intention driven by agency, emotivism, and in some cases, envy or vicious malice. There are plenty of public examples of high-profile people who have experienced *schadenfreude*. Hence, Eric Dezenhall earns his living in crisis management in public relations.

Envy is not a reaction to suffering but it is suffering, and *schadenfreude* is satisfaction from one's state of envy (Portmann, 2000, p. 18). Three conceptions of envy could be described as follows: (1) the resentment you grudge when you do not want others to have what you have, (2) the willingness to give up part of what you have to bring another person down, and (3) the desire to destroy what is good because you cannot have it yourself (Portmann, 2000, p. 19). These conceptions help us to understand the notion of agency and emotivism inherent in the acts of *schadenfreude*. Often we, the public receiving this spectacle of *schadenfreude*, fail to see or admit to these potential motives. Nevertheless, we sometimes passively accept these conditions without fully recognizing that what we witness is an act of *schadenfreude*. This discussion sought to provide a textured and layered understanding of *schadenfreude* and distinguish between American and German cultural implications of the concept itself. The rest of this chapter will be concerned about the American obsession with *schadenfreude* and finding an ethical response.

There are four stages of *schadenfreude* as articulated by Dezenhall:

Discovery—Someone rises to the occasion—fair-haired privileged-talented person.

Coronation—Someone gets extra attention in place of others.

Flaw detection—Someone is not all that he/she was made-out to be. A flaw—real, imagined or exaggerated is identified.

Humiliation—Someone is destroyed or evaluated more critically—often hunted. (p. 120)

These stages suggest that people can be chosen as targets of *schadenfreude* on the basis of their public or private actions. In addition, the flaw detection stage is where motives can go very wrong, as the truth can sometimes be distorted or fabricated. A more textured discussion of *schadenfreude* follows through three binary metaphorical considerations that assist in teasing out a more textured understanding of *schadenfreude*.

A Textured Understanding of *Schadenfreude*

Tensions in public realms related to provincial or cosmopolitan interests can be considered through dualistic metaphors of civility/incivility, agency/embeddedness, trust/skepticism. These are a "unity of contraries" (Arnett & Arneson, 1999, p. 142) that can help us to understand fully the complexities inherent in *schadenfreude*.

Civility/Incivility

In a *schadenfreude* experience, the lines between civility and incivility are blurred and often ambiguous. Sometimes the incivility of a person is masked by a false civility—presented as the vindicator who is really the catalyst of the attack. This person shrouds himself or herself in the righteous act of fixing what is wrong with the villain. As communicative exchanges turn to accusations and then to mudslinging, incivility is the paramount communicative gesture that occurs.

One concept of civility is to make a commitment to others that calls for respect to topics, issues, ideas, the historical moment, and a multiplicity of perspectives that abound in our postmodern world (Arnett & Arneson, 1999). If civility involves respect for others in communicative encounters, incivility would include those communicative actions that lack respect for others, falsehoods, or those empty words that intend to be ambiguous or noncommittal. In *schadenfreude,* incivility is routine and an unreflective communicative practice. Sometimes this lack of reflectiveness prohibits fair and just communicative exchanges. Consistent with the American understanding of *schadenfreude*, incivility can create hurtful, cynical, and negative communication between human beings. Although some cynicism is sometimes useful in negotiating communication between people (Arnett & Arneson, 1999), communication propelled by incivility can lead to very negative, hurtful, and debilitating communication of events and patterns. Incivility is often driven by agency. Agency and embeddedness are the next two dualistic metaphors that exemplify *schadenfreude.*

Agency/Embeddedness

People driven by agency can easily commit acts of *schadenfreude* because one's phenomenological focus of attention is positively grounded in the self and negatively grounded in perceptions of the other. *Schadenfreude* has been in existence since the documentation of human history, it reveals easily in a culture of narcissism (Lasch, 1979) and is easier to emerge in any given situation. Being driven by agency propels the manifestation of *schadenfreude* because agency fuels jealousy and reveals emptiness. When one is driven by agency, one's concern resides in the social comparison of one to the other, often rendering the agent with more self-doubt and envy of others. This in itself creates the notion to remove the threat to one's social place, which is the catalyst that invokes *schadenfreude.*

Quite often, perpetrators of *schadenfreude* are not reflective and critical enough to see how this develops and takes hold of communicative exchanges. Simply put, *schadenfreude* resides in agency, for any person embedded into a particular organization or interpersonal context cannot engage *schadenfreude.* Embeddedness allows the genuine turning toward the other in such a way that agency cannot emerge and survive. Embeddedness points toward the relationship, the "between" (Buber, 1965 p. 98), and the ethical implications of living relationships with an Other. Besides the tensions of civility/incivility and agency/embeddedness, the duality of trust and skepticism informs our understanding of *schadenfreude*.

Trust/Skepticism

In a culture of narcissism, trust is hard to find (Lasch, 1979). Ronald C. Arnett suggests that "loss of trust in common centers and moral stories [...] lays the groundwork for a survival mentality" (1994, p. 232). When we lose our common centers and moral stories, we lose a sense of place and our survival instinct emerges, opening up to emotivism and agency (Arnett, 1994; Lasch, 1984). Arnett (1994) argues that this emphasis on survival is what points human beings to attend to their own preferences; thereby we begin to be skeptical about everything other than what we know and create. The idea of being able to trust something becomes cynical and imbued with sarcasm.

In *schadenfreude*, there is no trust among attackers and no trust among the targets. In addition, the observers, we, those people who witness the attacks and witness the responses by the targets, become skeptical about what we see and how attacks are handled. We, the outsiders, begin to question motives of attackers, and secrets of the targets. To outsiders, we no longer trust in the truth of propositions by the attackers or the responses by the targets; *Schadenfreude* creates a culture of disbelief, neurosis, and uncertainty today therefore, we must consider the best ethical response possible to save the interiority of human thought and relationships.

Ethical Considerations of *Schadenfreude*

Immanuel Kant offers a perspective that can help us to understand ethics related to *schadenfreude* in a global sense. Kant argues that ethics has to do with actions that we do not do because we have to do them, but because the actions themselves are "in themselves right" and we are disposed to do them (Kant, 1963, p. 71). Kant lists duties toward others as

1. showing good will or benevolence

2. showing indebtedness or justice

3. having unconditional duties

4. showing respect for the rights of others. (p. 191)

Inherent in these duties toward others, Kant (1963) discusses, jealousy and its offspring also have a role to play. As we strive for perfection over others, we engage in social comparison. Once we socially compare what we have with what others have, we might develop a grudge. Kant (1963) argues that a grudge is "displeasure we feel when another has an advantage. This advantage makes us feel small and we grudge it him" (p. 217). This grudge does not fit in with Kant's frame of duty ethics. Typically, social comparison helps the grudge to develop. Quite often in *schadenfreude*, there is a grudge. Søren Kierkegaard offers hope for the provinciality of *schadenfreude* as his work opens up to application—how do we not fall prey to this action?

Søren Kierkegaard (1946) stated that there is "only one situation in which either/or has absolute significance, namely when truth, righteousness, and holiness are lined up on one side, and lust and base propensities and obscure passions and perdition on the other; yet it is always important to choose rightly" (p. 97). In the case of *schadenfreude*, Kierkegaard would suggest that at the very local level, it is a poor choice. When one treats another human being "superciliously, you make sport of them, and what you have become is what you most abhor...a universal critic" (p. 105). Kierkegaard suggests that this type of universal critic, in all areas of his or her life, is propelled by emotion and wants because choices are immediate and relative, and connected to one's own agency. To make an ethical decision one would reflect on issues in the realm of the aesthetical, in which one does not make a decision yet it is where one comes to a truth. Once the truth is "come to," one is able to move to the ethical realm and make a decision, volition, posit the best action, and then take it. In acts of *schadenfreude*, the acts are based on emotion and not a reflection unhampered by bias. Kierkegaard would argue that in regard to *schadenfreude*, the actor or attacker has not played enough in the aesthetical to come to a truth and allow for a truly ethical response. At a local, real-world, down-to-earth level, Kierkegaard reminds us that in any situation one must take these steps of reflection and action carefully and seriously or otherwise, risk acting within a schadenfreudistic paradigm. Sometimes, this emotionally charged response is most evident in smaller situations involving nonfamous persons, yet persons who carried much weight in a particular venue. The hope that Kierkegaard offers is that he reminds us to play in the aesthetical before we act in the world. This may likely ensure an ethical response.

Individuals ought to consider and be prepared to react and respond to acts of *schadenfreude* because we ought to have our own philosophy, especially in organizational communicative encounters, to deal with these types of attacks (Richardson, 2005). In fact, Kant would argue in favor of having a duty to respond in *schadenfreude*-laden acts (Timmermann, 2005). Yet, Kant is not sufficient in bringing a resolution to *schadenfreude*. His concepts help us to evaluate *schadenfreude* and enlarge our ability to strategize an ethical response (Hayry, 2005). Kierkegaard allows us to see the need for a local response because his ethics are less universal than Kant's and more specific in action.

Dissuasion: An Ethical Response

One might ask why we should respond to acts of *schadenfreude*. Moral concepts are embedded in and help to make up social life (MacIntyre, 1966/1998). If *schadenfreude* is part of social life (as it is), a morally grounded response to it is also part of that social life. Stephen Toulmin (1968) suggested that ethics relies on reasoning that is a "dialectical form" (p. 74). *Schadenfreude* demands a dialectical response grounded in a "correspondence theory of truth" (p. 74). The correspondence theory of truth simply suggests that a "proposition is 'true' [...when] it 'corresponds to a fact'" (p. 74). This locates the truth in the proposition, outside the speaker or the hearer. When propositions are exchanged in a dialectical form and truth is found in the conclusion of the propositions exchanged, an ethical response to *schadenfreude* is possible. This ethical response, in itself, is an act called "dissuasion" (Dezenhall, 1999, p. 199). In dissuasion, attackees fight back dialectically. Dissuasion is a stance, "an expanded mindset for convincing attackers to stop attacking or to not attack at all. It means GO AWAY" (pp. 200–201). Dissuasion is not a bag of tricks that allows the attackee to act at the same low level as the attackers. Rather, dissuasion is "an unconventional approach of limited tolerance and righteous indignation" (p. 201). Dissuasion does three things:

1. Introduces a risk to the attackers (why they shouldn't attack)
2. Transfers the subtext of malice to the attacker and removes it from the target
3. Inoculates the attackee from future attacks

In essence, dissuasion stops the attackers in their steps. By speaking the "truth" in a dialectical encounter, the attackee can end the assault simply by saying what "is." For example, if President Bill Clinton had said, "I did have sexual relations with that woman," instead of "I did not have sexual relations with that woman," his attackers would have nothing left to attack, except maybe to question the integrity of a president who cheats on his wife and lies about it to millions of people. Another example would be Michael Jackson. Had he not dangled the infant over the balcony railing, his credibility, integrity, and competency would not have been questioned and we might not see him as the target of multiple innuendo.

Grounded in emotion, not emotivism and truth, dissuasion is a type of dialectical advocacy that invites the exchange of information to get to a truth. *Schadenfreude* practitioners do not like dialectical advocacy because it has the power to stop them in their tracks and does not permit further negativity. In a sense, this is a way of playing ethical hardball. To let the attacker know that you will play this hardball and not let him or her get away with attacking you as a target is central to the effectiveness of it.

Dissuasion is dialectical, Dezenhall (1999) suggests, and is effectively based on emotion, not analysis. In the case of Clinton, had he said "I did have sexual relations with that woman," the public would react on emotion, potentially relating to fidelity in their own marriage as either the victim or the perpetrator. Two weeks later all might be forgotten. Instead, Clinton gave his attackers more rhetoric to analyze and evaluate against other testimony, which continued a negative dialectical exchange based within lies. So, while dissuasion stops the communicative attack, ultimately, it is an active communicative tool designed to stop future negative communicative attacks—not all-human communication in general. In addition, attackers are predictable, so to protect against *schadenfreude*, one can always not give the attackers something to talk about. Therefore, one should guard his or her business and communicative transactions accordingly. Dissuasion is moral posturing toward attackers (Dezenhall, 1999). Borrowing the concept of "practical philosophy" from Ronald C. Arnett (1990), dissuasion can make a difference in the impact it has on the human condition.

Hypothetical Exemplar

To demonstrate the particularities of this dialectical advocacy as a response to the negative form of *schadenfreude,* a hypothetical exemplar can be helpful. Consider this five-point discussion including an exemplar set-up, the scenario, an ethical response, the outcome, and implications/future considerations of this response.

Exemplar Set-Up

This exemplar can be set up through Dezenhall's six elements—victim, villain, vindicator, void, vehicle, and value. By identifying these elements we can better understand the act of *schadenfreude* that occurs. In this very common case exemplar, the act of *schaden-freude* occurs within an organization that is part of higher educa-tion. Consider any academic department in any college or university setting in which there are a variety of impressions and understand-ings of the nature of scholarship. Depending on where faculty attend graduate school, influences from mentors, individual work ethic, individual situatedness of one's life phase, and multiple connotations of what constitutes scholarship can emerge. Thus, these perspectives can stir up ill feelings between different human beings and thwart camaraderie—almost pitting one against the other. In the case where *schadenfreude* emerges, instances of verbal attacks, both public and private, may occur, a questioning or out-right insubordination might occur relative to decisions and simple daily practices. Other attacks pertaining to scholarship and one's basic reputation might also surface, and there could be institutional sabotage in which one person might begin to bad talk or conspire with others to give faulty or fraudulent information to higher ad-ministrators who have the power to negatively impact any faculty member's experience and job in general. All these components tell one tale of potential *schadenfreude* in the academy; however, the circumstances are easily transferable to any other organizational paradigm.

More specifically, Dezenhall's six elements can be broken down in this way in this hypothetical exemplar:

Victim—Untenured faculty member who will be applying for tenure in two years.

Villain—A tenured faculty member in department for eight years who has published two books, several articles he or she is preparing to be chair of department in the next semester.

Vindicator—A tenured faculty member from another department.

Void—The need to bring clarity into tenure requirements and the question of whether or not tenure should be comparable for all faculty at the same institution.

Vehicle—Rumor mill, dean, and potentially the school newspaper.

Value—The principle of academic freedom.

The scenario describes the actual circumstance of *schadenfreude* and the implications that arise to individuals, the academic community, and the public at large.

Scenario

In this particular department the tenure requirements are relatively ambiguous, yet people seem to know intuitively how to prepare for tenure consideration. In this exemplar, tension arises as the "victim" believes the "villain" is being unreasonable in his or her consideration of tenure as he or she holds particular criteria that are more rigorous than the previous chair held. Specifically, the outgoing chair based his or her tenure recommendations on personality rather than a set criteria that can be fairly and equally implemented across department personnel. In addition, as the criteria will be written and therefore less ambiguous, the potential for legal matters between tenure candidates and the institution can be reduced. In the past, there had been legal action taken against the institution because of the lack of tenure clarity and set criteria to support other faculty being fired. The "villain" is charged with the task of better clarifying departmental standards for tenure.

It is in this charge that problems begin to arise and the "victim" begins to feel pressure for not pursuing a component of service and scholarship in his or her academic experience up to this point. The incoming chair or "villain" must set forth tenure criteria and give the "victim" opportunity to begin to demonstrate activity in these areas. The problem is that the "victim" is happy with not doing service and not working on scholarship for conference presentations or scholarly publications. When the incoming chair or the "villain" sets the criteria and does not waiver for one person, *schadenfreude* emerges in a very public way.

The "victim" begins to talk about the "villain" behind the back and propel a rumor-laden character attack that cannot be substantiated. The "victim" argues that conference presentations should not be a requirement but rather an option. Likewise, the "victim" argues that publishing in journals should not be required criteria and that composing messages on public blogs should be an alternative to peer-reviewed publications. The "victim" begins to not only propel rumors against the "villain," but he/she also begins to lie and speak for others in the department so that administrators and other faculty from any department might think that all faculty in the particular department agree and feel the same way—but this is only a rumor and, again, it is not the truth.

Once these schadenfreudistic actions are in place, the other faculty members in the department take note of them and realize that someone is using their names to promote an agency-driven perspective. While some faculty might agree with the "victim," others do not agree and thus starts a widespread disagreement with a focal point of questioning the ethos of the "villain" or, more colloquially, trashing his/her reputation in the academy.

The "villain" can approach this situation in a variety of ways that can be helpful or hurtful. This chapter would argue that "dissuasion" or dialectical advocacy is one approach that can stop the rumor mill and reveal truth, while getting at the root of the problem and ending this dialectical negativity and the potential diabolic attack. A "vindicator" enters the game as the entity who will correct this error. In this case, the vindicator would be administrators who should be impartial but they also have biases and their own perspective that may not fully assist the ability to quell *schadenfreude*. The "vehicle" of this attack seems to grow. First, the rumor mill is set in motion through a verbal forum, and then the discussion enters the personal blog of the "victim" that is a public forum because it is available to anyone who has Internet access. When the issues get to the administrator's offices, then more formal vehicles are utilized, such as administrative memos or other such documents. In addition, if the "victim" becomes so public with his/her demands or accusations, the school newspaper may report this unfavorable situation to its audience. Therefore, print media, the Internet, and word of mouth are at least three potential vehicles that this situation might encounter.

Finally, the "value" that the "victim" might hide behind is the idea of academic freedom that is closely tied to the tenure discussion (Hofstadter & Smith, 1961; O'Neil, 1999). Instead of announcing to the world that one doesn't want to put the time into developing scholarship or volunteering service for the institution, one can argue that a particular set criteria might interfere with the philosophy of academic freedom. This exemplar set-up should provide at least some insight into how *schadenfreude* emerges in organizations and between human beings, as well as what propels it. Finding an ethical response is important so that negative and deceitful information does not shape communicative decision making.

Ethical Response

Eric Dezenhall suggests that the responsive action of "dissuasion" will stop *schadenfreude* from propelling beyond the initial impact. By engaging in this dialectical advocacy, negative communicative exchanges cease and truthful or perhaps even accurate communicative exchanges can emerge. In this exemplar, dissuasion would invite public discussion at faculty meetings regarding the rumor mill issues and individual perspectives on tenure and the idea of academic freedom. By inviting discussion pertaining to what these issues mean to each faculty member, revelations can emerge that individuals might not have originally considered. These revelations can come to any or all participants—not just the "victim" who is the actual *schadenfreude* perpetrator. Dissuasion confronts the attacker in a moral jujitsu, so to speak, because it reveals truth and invites open forum discussion rather than backroom or closed-door rumor proliferation.

Another ethical response of the target of *schadenfreude* should be to not give any further ammunition to the actor propelling *schadenfreude*. This is the responsibility of the target—to be guided by a particular ethical paradigm in everyday communicative action. So by not giving the attacker anything to attack, by publicly stating and demonstrating your actions so that administrators can see your approach and work ethic, and by inviting the notion of dialectical advocacy between you and your attackers, *schadenfreude* becomes impotent and negative consequences can be dispelled.

Outcome

Truth should prevail—but we know that it doesn't always surface. Dissuasion is dialectical advocacy that is an Aristotelian approach to get at a truth and reveal the untruths of a given situation. This is one way of approaching communicative exchanges that reveal truths in a public manner—thus providing the opportunity to dispel the lies and potentially reveal agency-driven agendas of others.

If the target of *schadenfreude* speaks her mind, so will others. For one person or a select few people to speak for others fraudulently because of their own agency-driven agenda, the lives, reputations, and careers of others can be destroyed. Stopping *schadenfreude* in its tracks can reveal truths and limit exploitation by others. Isn't it time that people speak up and out against these often vicious attacks by the few?

Implications and Future Considerations

Consideration of dialectical advocacy in the frame of dissuasion shows that it is easy to get at a truth in a story through communication driven by the story and not individual agency. Through the dialectical advocacy of dissuasion, hidden agendas can be revealed and thwarted. Reasoning that emerges between the participants of dissuasive dialectical advocacy can paint a completely new picture that neither participant considered, and by being so public about the situation, there is less risk of one side acting from selfish reasons and propelling rumors or other destructive behavior.

Dialectical advocacy in the guise of dissuasion calls forth to (1) find new ways to think about public communication because *schadenfreude* manifests in a public manner, (2) consider how agency drives motives and how it can affect organizational communication, (3) look at how *schadenfreude* affects not only high-profile celebrities but also the everyday common human agent, (4) explore other connotations of *schadenfreude* like the layers of connotation of *schadenfreude* within the German culture, (5) bring attention to *schadenfreude* in the marketplace to help people to have a better understanding of it and plan for an ethical response, and finally (6) announce to those human agents who engage *schadenfreude* either knowingly or unknowingly, "Stop It." Understanding our actions ourselves can help us to think differently about what motivates us and how we engage others. Understanding *schadenfreude* better can help us to be better communicators ourselves.

There are many potential implications for this topic of inquiry because this is a critique of communicative action, and our field has not fully considered implications of *schadenfreude*. One significant area of impact that this chapter offers is that whether we are in a culture of attack or not, we still see attacks of public people in a global setting and attacks of private people in local settings. In the American sense, *schadenfreude* is a communicative strategy designed to be hurtful toward others. To enhance communicative responses and move human communication toward a more ethical model, we ought to consider future inquiry into this form of communication that requires crisis management public relations practitioners to respond to something. Not everyone is nice. The communication discipline holds the expertise and skill in helping to recognize these subpar forms of human communication as well as the alternative approaches to engagement in these forms of communication. In thinking about communication ethics, we should consider ethical responses to communicative conditions that fall short of maintaining human dignity.

References

Anonymous. (2003). Could it happen to us? *Economist*, 368 (8338), 17.

Arnett, R. C. (1990). The practical philosophy of communication ethics and free speech as the foundation for speech communication. *Communication Quarterly*, 38 (3), 208–217.

———. (1994). Existential homelessness: A contemporary case for dialogue. In Rob Anderson, Kenneth Cissna & Ronald C. Arnett (Eds.), *The reach of dialogue: Confirmation, voice, and community*. Cresskill, NJ: Hampton Press.

Arnett, R.C., & Arneson, P. (1999). *Dialogic civility in a cynical age: Community, hope, and interpersonal relationships*. Albany: State University of New York Press.

Buber, M. (1965). *Between man and man*. New York: Macmillan.

Dezenhall, E. (1999). *Nail'em: Confronting high-profile attacks on celebrities and businesses*. New York: Prometheus Books.

Hayry, M. (2005). The tension between self governance and absolute inner worth in Kant's moral philosophy. *Journal of Medical Ethics*, 31, 645–647.

Hofstadter, R., & Smith, W. (1961). *American higher education: A documentary history*. Chicago, IL: University of Chicago Press.

Kafka, F. (1992). *Brief an den vater* (Letters to my father). Frankfurt: Fischer.

Kant, I. (1956). *Critique of pure reason*. (L. W. Beck, Trans.). Indianapolis, IN: Bobbs-Merrill.

———. (1963). *Lectures on ethics.* New York: Harper Torchbooks.

Kierkegaard, S. (1946). Either/Or. In Robert Bretall (Ed.), *A Kierkegaard Anthology* (19–108). Princeton, NJ: Princeton University Press.

Lasch, C. (1979). *The culture of narcissism: American life in an age of diminishing expectations.* New York: Norton.

———. (1984). *The minimal self: Psychic survival in troubled times.* New York: Norton.

Leach, C. W., Spears, R., Branscombe, N., & Doosje, B. (2003). Malicious pleasure: Schadenfreude at the suffering of another group. *Journal of Personality and Social Psychology,* 84 (5), 932–943.

MacIntyre, A. (1966/1998). *A short history of ethics: A history of moral philosophy from the Homeric age to the twentieth century.* Notre Dame, IN: University of Notre Dame Press.

O'Neil, R. M. (1999). Academic freedom past, present, and future. In Philip G. Altbach, Robert O. Berdahl & Patricia Gumport (Eds.), *American higher education in the twenty-first century: Social, political, and economic challenges.* Baltimore: Johns Hopkins University Press.

Peverley, P. (2005). Schadenfreude. *Pulse,* 65(23), 30.

Portmann, J. (2000). *When bad things happen to other people.* New York: Routledge.

Richardson, B.F. (2005). Developing a personal philosophy on organizational ethics and wrongdoing. *Texas Speech Communication Journal,* 30 (1), 81–83.

Rushin, S. (2002). The ecstasy of defeat. *Sports Illustrated,* 97(11), 23.

Timmermann, J. (2005). Good but not required?—Assessing the demands of Kantian ethics. *Journal of Moral Philosophy,* 2 (1), 9–27.

Toulmin, S. J. (1968). *An examination of the place of reason in ethics.* Cambridge: Cambridge University Press.

Zagorin, P. (2000). The joys of schadenfreude. *Virginia Quarterly Review,* 76, 546–550.

Chapter 2

Political Communication and Ethical "Celebrity Advocacy"

Melissa A. Cook

Social and political advocacy offered by celebrities has been pervading American social and political causes for at least the past 50 years. This chapter makes a concentrated effort to consider the metaphor celebrity advocacy to explain ethical communication positioned by a "celebrity" in favor of a particular social issue, a political issue, or a specific political nominee. Many times the public will look at these celebrities in very polarizing ways, either for or against the platform the celebrity is advocating. The public asks why attention should be paid to an actor discussing politics, just because they have the stage. The answer can be found in the form of narrative communicative efforts. If the activism is part of a larger story that has veracity and substance, the advocacy can be viewed as ethical communication.

Celebrity advocacy played the role of a central character in the story of the 2004 U.S. presidential election, especially during the last weeks of the campaign. Celebrities such as singer/song writer Bruce Springsteen lent his voice to the John Kerry presidential campaign during the "Vote for Change" tour. The tour occurred in October 2004 with shows presented in "swing states" by Springsteen and more than a dozen other musical artists including The Dixie Chicks, James Taylor, and REM. This type of celebrity advocacy concerned politics and the support of a very specific candidate. At times this type of advocacy could occur for a particular party during an election cycle or a political/social issue with legal ramifications.

This type of political/social issue can be exemplified in the case of stem cell research and the celebrity who advocates for its legal acceptance at the national legislative level, actor Michael J. Fox. Owing to his own debilitating illness of Parkinson's disease, Fox has been a vocal advocate for embryonic stem cell research on Capitol Hill, realizing he might not find a cure in time for himself, but wanting to help future victims of these types of illnesses and spinal injuries that may be assisted with the help of stem cell research. At the end of the election cycle in 2006, Fox was interviewed although his disease-induced body tremors were very apparent, in an attempt to show the audience the true external effects of his disease. Fox's actions were debated on the eve of the midterm elections, with a particularly popular syndicated talk radio host suggesting the actor was acting and that Fox purposely didn't take his medication for effect (Montgomery, 2006, p. C01).

In different camps, these celebrity advocates are celebrated and in others they are told to "shut up and sing,"[1] for instance. Analyzing the competing narratives that surrounded these various artists and their fan base and the decision making of the electorate through a variety of philosophical and ethical paradigms permits fruitful discussion about debate. This chapter considers whether public communication by public personalities/celebrities in support or opposition of public issues or political matters, which I term celebrity advocacy, weakens or strengthens debate within a democracy charged with crucial decision-making duties. Using the work of renowned narrative theorist Alasdair MacIntyre, this chapter explores the persuasive impact of celebrity advocacy in the context of political and legislative advocacy and offers pragmatic discussion for the usefulness of celebrity advocacy found within narrative contexts.

Introduction

Different philosophical perspectives on communication ethics may constructively address choices confronting organizations at the macro level as well as decision making at the personal level. These decisions may be inside and/or outside specific organizations or even at the micro level, within families or personal decisions. This chapter explores the effects of ethical communicative advocacy on decision making in the private and public political processes. This study of communication ethics is united with a premier contemporary philosopher to engage communication ethics from a praxis orientation.

Celebrities have been politicking for many decades, especially since the rise of the various media outlets that would give the celebrity a stage/platform for their voice. Famed singer Frank Sinatra stumped[2] for presidential nominee John Kennedy and eventually for fellow actor and presidential nominee Ronald Reagan, while President Richard Nixon had Sammy Davis Jr. as an advocate in the 1960s (Carpenter, 2004). Those who thought the 2004 Vote for

Change tour was the first major grouping of artists would be mistaken, since the 1968 campaign had acts and "Simon & Garfunkel, Janis Joplin, Creedence Clearwater Revival and John Sebastian headlined a concert for Democratic Candidate Eugene McCarthy at Shea Stadium" (Carpenter, 2004, p. 3). Carpenter suggests that the 2004 tour seems different because the celebrities used various media outlets and we have the Internet, now. "And whether it's television, radio, film or visual art, most artistic political expression is mostly left-leaning in content" (Carpenter, 2004, p. 5).

Celebrities have often endorsed political parties or politicians in particular in the past century and have become spokespeople for a multitude of nonprofit organizations hoping to gain attention through the use of celebrity endorsement. Donna Freydkin (2006) discusses celebrity activities in the newspaper *USA Today* when she emphasized Audrey Hepburn's work with UNICEF, Bob Hope's association with UFO Shows for American Troops abroad and at home, and Elizabeth Taylor as one of the first major actors to discuss AIDS in public statements. However, this election was different; there was something in the air that hinted toward a rhetorical interruption (Hyde, 2001, p. 78). This election mattered on many different fronts, especially the war front, and Americans were split down the middle. This presidential election was going to be another close contest between incumbent President George W. Bush and democratic challenger Senator John Kerry of Massachusetts. This election was a dividing point for the country.

Defeating the Incumbent

After eight years of a Democratic-run White House, Republican nominee George W. Bush won the 2000 presidential election with more electoral college votes, defeating the sitting Vice President Al Gore, who won the popular vote. The contest was so close that the results of the election were fought all the way to the Supreme Court. Gore finally conceded the election almost five weeks after election night (CNN.com). President George W. Bush was running the country when three commercial aircrafts were used on September 11, 2001, to assault the United States in a form of terrorism never before seen on U.S. soil. The world was witness to the World Trade Towers crashing to the ground early that fateful morning, as television cameras were held steady on the buildings following the first plane's initial and purposeful crash into one of the towers in Lower

Manhattan, New York. Then the media announced another attack on the Pentagon and a third plane that was on its way, probably toward the White House, went crashing to the earth in Shanksville, a small town in southwestern Pennsylvania, following what was later determined to be a passenger assault on the terrorists that caused the plane to possibly crash earlier than planned. The pilots of the aircrafts were terrorists, with the plan masterminded by Osama bin Ladin, leader of al Qaeda.

The National Commission on Terrorist Attacks Upon the United States (2004) explained the decision to attack those responsible for the strikes on Americans:

> The State Department proposed delivering an ultimatum to the Taliban: produce Bin Ladin and his deputies and shut down al Qaeda camps within 24 to 48 hours, or the United States will use all necessary means to destroy the terrorist infrastructure. The State Department did not expect the Taliban to comply. Therefore, State and Defense would plan to build an international coalition to go into Afghanistan. Both departments would consult with NATO and other allies and request intelligence, basing, and other support from countries, according to their capabilities and resources. Finally, the plan detailed a public U.S. stance: America would use all its resources to eliminate terrorism as a threat, punish those responsible for the 9/11 attacks, hold states and other actors responsible for providing sanctuary to terrorists, work with a coalition to eliminate terrorist groups and networks, and avoid malice toward any people, religion, or culture. (10.2)

It was determined that the Taliban was harboring bin Laden, and since they denied having him, the United States invaded Afghanistan. Later, President Bush announced that Iraq was hiding weapons of mass destruction (WMD), and the U.S. military invaded Iraq to remove their leader President Saddam Hussein. Though it has been corroborated that Hussein used WMD on his own people, the Kurds, no large stockpiles that would be of a threat to the rest of the world, were ever found. In December 2003, eight months after the fall of Bagdad to U.S. forces, Hussein was eventually found by U.S. military ("Saddam," www.BBC.com, 2003). Hussein was sentenced to death by his own government and hanged on December 30, 2006 (Knickmeyer, 2006).

From all of the constant media coverage in Afghanistan and Iraq, it was announced and believed that the United States had effectively succeeded in entering these countries and completing their various goals, and that the United States had "won." However, the problems had only begun. The U.S. military was still in Afghanistan, and Iraq in particular, on the eve of the 2004 presidential election, and evidence began to surface that Iraq did not have WMD. The campaign rhetoric that followed announced that Americans were "lied to."

One of the main issues of the 2004 election, then, was about the war in Iraq. Though exit polls showed a strong lean toward "family values," going into election on Tuesday, the country thought it was voting on the war and terrorism (beliefnet.com). Enter Bruce Springsteen and his celebrity advocacy. Springsteen was staunchly against the continued fight in Iraq, and though he supported the troops, he argued for a change in the White House so that there would be a change in the war.

In August 2004, it was announced that a few bands would assemble in various groupings to offer concerts around the country, and only in "swing" states (states that were too close to call on the eve of the election, and that could "swing" the results in one direction or another). The Vote for Change tour had a few different versions of political rhetoric, with some acts suggesting the tour was about getting out the vote, and there needed to be a regime change in the White House.

Vote for Change Tour 2004

Springsteen was stumping for an actual candidate, in Democrat John Kerry, as opposed to simply promoting the Democratic Party in general, as he had throughout most of his career, especially at the height of his popularity in the 1980s with the album *Born in the U.S.A.* Over the past three decades, Springsteen's music has been about the working-class man/woman, who needed to work hard to have a bit of success, if they were lucky, search for love and perhaps fall in love and continue to work hard. The partisanship Springsteen adhered to on the Vote for Change tour put his reputation to the test. In the past, he had not backed any one particular candidate, and now he was on stage suggesting to both fans and nonfans alike who to support on Election Day.

The communication espoused in celebrity advocacy is proper and ethical if it follows a path of what has come before or what has been said before. Springsteen's music has always been filled with liberal lyrics that resonate in albums such as *Nebraska* and *Born in the U.S.A.* What was ironic was that *Born in the U.S.A.* was co-opted by President Ronald Reagan in September 1984 although Springsteen was at the beginning of what came to be the height of his popularity, filling outdoor stadiums the following summer on the success of his album *Born in the U.S.A.* Springsteen even mentions the irony in concert during late September 1984, and questioned whether Reagan understood the album at all.

A *New York Times* opinion piece by Joe Margolis (2004), a former political reporter, suggested that "Campaigns are won or lost depending on what is happening in the world and how effectively the candidates campaign. Popular culture is just a postmodern term for entertainment, which is a lot more fun than politics, but totally different" (A21). Springsteen and guests on the tour felt that they could entertain and discuss politics at the same time. Some fans weren't having it!

Dave Marsh (2006), longtime biographer of Springsteen, explained that if fans were unsure as to why Springsteen joined forces for change in the White House in 2004, then those fans must not have listened "acutely" to "20 years of supporting the homeless and the hungry, about thirty years of stories about growing up poor, *No Nukes, The Ghost of Tom Joad* and '41 Shots'" (p. 284). Marsh is alluding to Springsteen's lyrical themes; concert storytelling; Springsteen's appearance at the 1979 concerts promoting the dangers of nuclear energy; a solo album-*Joad*, dedicated to the plight of the migrant worker in America; and finally the song written during a 1999 Springsteen & band reunion tour, "41 Shots," that questioned three New York City cops and their firing 41 bullets at "an unarmed African man" (Marsh, 2006, p. 241). Amadou Diallo, lying dead in the vestibule of a Bronx apartment building, was found to be unarmed and probably reaching for his identification when ordered to stop running by the police. Marsh's point is obvious to the Springsteen fan of multiple decades. Perhaps not quite so obvious, however, were Springsteen's actions to anyone simply familiar with the famed *Born in the U.S.A.* album of the 1980s or the person who "danced in the dark" with Monica from *Friends*.[3]

During his tour to major sports venues of the mid-1980s, Springsteen was known to give $10,000 to local food pantries in each city he visited, and always asked his fans to bring canned goods to help stock those pantries. He also recognized the plight of Vietnam veterans and was a supporter for their well-being. Springsteen's writings, stories, and actions all supported the very thing he was fighting for in 2004–a change for the common man, the uselessness of war, and a just America at the end of the day. The 2004 presidential election was so close that Springsteen called Senator Kerry, telling him he would support Kerry during the week before the election. Kerry took his offer, and Springsteen accompanied him for a week during very strategic geographically planned Kerry rallies. Springsteen played a few songs with his acoustic guitar, offered a "public service announcement" about why he was campaigning with Kerry, and then, finally introduced the next president of the United States during these rallies. The men appeared together up until the eve of the election, from Wisconsin to Florida and eventually to Ohio–and what became the swing state Kerry needed 24 hours later, but never received.

At the end of the day, none of the swing states swung. Wisconsin had been close and went for Kerry, a testament, perhaps to the 80,000 people who came out at the capitol for a Springsteen/Kerry stop. But, the most important state, at the end of election night and into the Wednesday morning of election week, Ohio became a question–mark–it could have gone either way by the late evening of Tuesday Election and some Americans went to bed not knowing the outcome of the presidential election. Ohio did stay "red," and Senator Kerry was defeated by the incumbent President Bush ("Ohio," WashingtonPost.com, 2004).

Will This Celebrity Advocacy Assist Decision Making?

Celebrity advocacy seems to be accepted more when physical ailments and social issues are at stake, such as the work Michael J. Fox is doing for stem cell research. Bono, lead singer for the internationally acclaimed Irish rock band U2, has also been held in high regard. He has given of his time to travel the world to talk with leaders to assist with the prevention and treatment of AIDS, especially in Africa and debt relief for third world countries. In discussing the bigger issues Bono tackles, Jon Soeder (2005) interviewed the chief curator for the Rock and Roll Hall of Fame, Jim Henke, who explained, "Bono's activism is a natural extension of the band's socially conscious brand of anthemic rock" (p. 1).

Because of their high status in popular culture, and the fame that follows them, celebrities are able to open doors. They can garner support from their typical fan base to rally around a cause or action. Singer/songwriter Dave Matthews quoted in *Rolling Stone*

(Fricke, 2004b), explained that though his road crew has many Republicans in the group, his band's decision to participate in the 2004 Vote for Change tour makes sense: "Our touring family is very close. But, just as we understand their position, they understand it's our prerogative to use the platform we have built to say whatever we want" (pp. 37-38). Many celebrities use that stage to go out on the proverbial limb and give advice, offer support, and make demands, at times, of their fans and potential fan base.

Many issues that would have otherwise been unnoticed come to the forefront of the discussion when a celebrity endorses a candidate/cause. We often see sound bites on the news of celebrities testifying before the U.S. Congress. Advocates such as actor Michael J. Fox have appeared in front of Congress, asking for support on their cause du jour. Are these people the most knowledgeable about the subject? Maybe, as in the case of Fox, he has the disease and has become engrossed in raising funds and public awareness about the disease, not to benefit him as much as future generations. He supports stem cell research and any candidate who will also support the legislation required for scientists to use the coveted stem cells.

During the 2004 midterm election, Fox decided to speak in a commercial to support a particular candidate who was a stem cell supporter. Rush Limbaugh went on the attack on his radio program, suggesting that Fox purposely did not take his medicine so that the audience would be more sympathetic to his pleas. In a news article discussing his second book, Fox explained the event in 2004 and the impact on the news cycle:

> Our goal was to educate voters about the stem cell issue and what was there to be accomplished and what had been forsaken with the current policy, but the nature of the counterattack was such that it opened up a whole secondary conversation which was about the level of discourse in political matters and other matters of social importance. The attack was so ad hominem it was jarring to people. (Seccombe, 2007)

Fox's first book, *Lucky Man* (2002), explained that once he came to terms with his disease he educated himself and made friends with many researchers and has made more progress toward a cure than government and other private research institutions. Fox believes that in his lifetime there could be a cure—but that stem cell research is the roadblock limiting this success.

Do the celebrities have a stake in the issues? Usually. And guess what–they have the audience. These issues may not have otherwise been articulated, or come before Congress anytime soon. So, do we listen to these celebrities? Do we put much credence in what they say? It depends, and their rhetoric should be weighed against their past actions, and knowledge on the subject at hand. It depends on the narrative in which they ground their rhetoric.

Philosophy of Communication: Communication Ethics and Narrative

A philosophy for everyday experiences is apparent in the action of the "doing" of communication ethics, in that philosophical theory can inform the daily praxis of communicators. Within a narrative, one can find a unifying theme that offers an overarching opportunity for coherence within stories. Internationally respected philosopher Alasdair MacIntyre has created a body of scholarly work around the themes of moral philosophy as well as religion and politics. His work on narrative assists this discussion regarding celebrity advocacy and how decisions are made within political communicative events.

Narrative

Alasdair MacIntyre (1981/1984) suggests that virtues will lead to the unity of a human life if grounded within a tradition. In defining the premodern concept of virtues, it is necessary to say something about the accompanying "concept of selfhood, a concept of a self whose unity resides in the unity of a narrative which links birth to life to death as narrative beginning to middle to end" (MacIntyre, 1981/1984, p. 205). MacIntyre suggests that virtues should be situated within the concept of finding "the good life for man and not only in relation to practices" (p. 220). If we think about postmodern decision making in times of elections, we see the democratic process bring the good life to fruition, through the process of choice making, electing men and women to run our country, at the macro level of government, or our community at the micro level.

Through communication we can realize our ethical selves. In postmodern times, our behavior is somewhat controlled by the social situations in which we find ourselves. Alasdair MacIntyre (1981/1984) suggests that it is through a narrative that one finds him/herself emerged within a rule-bound community. MacIntyre (1981/1984) explains, "behavior is only characterized adequately when we know what the longer and longest term intentions involved are and how the short term intentions are related to the longer. Therefore, we are writing a narrative history" (p. 208). Communication ethics, then, is the praxis of the philosophy of the Ancients to the Moderns, as MacIntyre explains, a type of "intelligibility" for which we can be held accountable for which only we (humans) are the authors (1981/1984, p. 209).

Therefore, speech becomes intelligible in a narrative and the purpose and speech acts require context (MacIntyre, 1981/1984) within which intelligibility will become obvious and make sense and the intelligibility will be "the conceptual connecting link between the notion of action and that of narrative" (MacIntyre, 1981/1984, p. 214). In terms of Springsteen's foray into not only politics, but actual support of one particular candidate, it makes sense for most fans of his music/lyrics, as Springsteen has been writing in the same context for three decades. Middle-class, working hero works hard for his small pay, but he has the girl at the end of the day. However, for others, the narrative didn't matter; it was the celebrity issue that bothered the electorate. What right did a singer have to offer political advice?

When Alasdair MacIntyre (1981/1984) discusses narratives in *After Virtue*, he does so to suggest that one is always coauthor of his or her own story, but one is also under certain constraints. "A central thesis begins to emerge: man is in his actions and practice, as well as in his fictions, essentially a story-telling animal. [. . .] through his history, a teller of stories that aspire to truth" (p. 216). MacIntyre (1981/1984) explains how the individual is the subject of the narrative in that the narratives are concepts of selfhood, in which "I am the subject of a history that is my own and no one else's, that has its own peculiar meaning" and second, correlatively "I am not only accountable, but I can ask others for an account, I am part of their story, they are part of mine," (p. 218). The storytelling nature of Springsteen's music/lyrics has never strayed. Springsteen biographer Dave Marsh (2006) explains that the songwriter's lyrical writings

> owe an increasing debt to literary sources...In part, it's because he's un-
> afraid of tacking big, important subjects that are ordinarily not discussed
> in song and, when they are, are usually reduced to agitprop, caricature, or
> incoherence. The clarity and psychological insight of his lyrics are beauti-
> ful, startling, and for many, profoundly moving, because they bespeak the

human heart as keenly as an earlier generation of music writers believed
that only educated musicians could. (pp. 11-12)

The contention here is that if the audience had followed the stories Springsteen wrote in his songs, the decision he made to support
our particular candidate (John Kerry) was because he wrote against
war, against lying and cheating. It only made sense that this advocacy would be the next step with his public and private persona.

Along with narratives, Alasdair MacIntyre (1981/1984) points to
traditions as holding families and communities together. A person
is part of a family who will inherit a "moral starting point" (p. 220).
The thought of one's past influencing one's morals is contrasted
with Modernism's individualistic thinking, "I am what I choose to
be." Exercises of virtue strengthen traditions and keep those traditions from disappearing, whereas a lack of virtues corrupts traditions (MacIntyre, 1981/1984, p. 223). Our practices are embedded
in history, "the history of a practice in our time is generally and
characteristically embedded in and made intelligible in terms of the
larger and longer history of the tradition through which the practice
in its present form was conveyed to us [. . .]" (1981/1984, p. 222).
Jack Russell Weinstein (2003) explains the importance of the connection between ethics and the traditions in which one is not only
raised, but also continues to live within:

> MacIntyre convinces his readers that morality is inseparable from cultural
> heritage, and that different ways of reasoning-different ways of thinking-
> are in constant conflict. He describes a world in which rival moral systems
> struggle to survive and to overshadow their competitors, and one in which
> beliefs can only be defended by appealing to important texts, sacred scrip-
> tures, and lengthy histories. (p. iv)

This connection of communication ethics, history, culture, and
reasoning is investigated in this work because of the movement
found within postmodernity to understand multiple narratives
working within our world.

In his seminal work on narration as a communication paradigm,
Walter Fisher (1984) clarifies that, by narration, he is referring "to a
theory of symbolic actions–words and/or deeds–that have sequence
and meaning for those who live, create, or interpret them" (p. 2).
Extrapolating this idea of narrative to organizations, the culture
can enable decisions to be made with good reasons and a narrative

rationality–a type of fidelity that can be used to evaluate organizational stories. If a story has fidelity, it includes loyalty, faithfulness, reliability, trustworthiness, dependability, devotion, commitment, and conformity.

On the basis of one's embedded history and the culture found within the environment of a narrative, decisions should be made within the horizon of significance (Gadamer, 2002) of the mission of the organization. "Coherent" (Fisher, 1984, p. 8) stories need to be a part of the mix when talking within an organizational setting. Those telling logical, sound, and consistent stories will base those stories on an embedded history and a culture found within the environment of a narrative.

As an organization grows and stories are told, it is natural for there to be a quest for the organization's continuous evolution. People will naturally want an organization to evolve. However, it should evolve within the framework of the overarching mission (narrative) of the organization. If one wants to change that mission dramatically, then ethical dialogue should ensue in an open environment where all can equally share in the discussion. The problems occur when those discussions are held in the "backroom" and without full participation. Springsteen and the artists who gave their time for the Vote for Change tour saw the Bush administration as one that was not forthcoming and had faltered in leading our nation. The ethics of such communication, to constituents, to potential voters is a crucial dynamic for investigation in this historical moment.

Communication Ethics

It is not only important to discuss the theory in philosophical communication but it is also necessary to put the information into practice, and communication ethics is a way that scholars can write about the need for a praxis orientation. A crucial component of communication ethics is investigating how society communicates and the methods and media used. Communication ethics cannot be studied in the abstract.

In his well-respected survey and analysis *A Short History of Ethics*, Alasdair MacIntyre (1998) looks at the communicative aspects of the community based on philosophers who were writing during various time periods–from ancient times to classic, to medieval to Enlightenment, and then modern times. MacIntyre suggests that history is an important part/piece of moral concepts. This is why the celebrity advocacy of Bruce Springsteen is significant to this historical moment. On the basis of the historical trend that Springsteen's work followed, his own writings and musings about the plight of the average American, it seems real as well as justified to be against an administration that contradicts everything you've announced as being true to you for the past 30 years. Moreover, these musings have been public! It isn't someone coming out on stage that is new to popular culture; it was a rock and roll legend in his own time, announcing that things have changed, and the administration was heading down a path he could not, in good conscience, agree with, especially now that he had children who will be around for the future.

Communication ethics become the praxis (theory informed action) of philosophy of communication. This discussion, then moves from MacIntyre's theory into implementation in practical, everyday interactions. This discussion is not engaging, nor working within a relativistic posture, nor being anachronistic. We are engaging questions within a given historical moment to enlighten this historical moment of postmodernity. Communication ethics allow us this glimpse into our decision making.

Jack Russell Weinstein (2003) argues that MacIntyre's connection of history to philosophy is important to study in tandem with morality. "MacIntyre convinces his readers that morality is inseparable from cultural heritage, and that different ways of reasoning–different ways of thinking–are in constant conflict" (p. iv). MacIntyre's use of praxis informs communication ethics, as communication is a form of praxis for ethics. How one lives one's life, especially in the public eye, is weighed and dissected in today's popular culture.

Another point that needs to be made regarding parameters around this work includes the realization that there is, indeed, a lack of insight into vernacular voices found in the writing of Alasdair MacIntyre's work on the history of ethics. MacIntyre (1998) focuses his work on and in the West, beginning *A Short History of Ethics* with the ancient Greeks and concluding with continental and a few American scholars. MacIntyre does not enter his work through Egypt, India, Asia, nor Islamic or Jewish religions. MacIntyre set his own parameters and worked within them, as he noted in his preface to the second edition of *A Short History of Ethics*. There is obviously room and a need for investigation of ethics in the East, and feminist ethics, for example, but this work will stay true to the work of MacIntyre as a guiding focal point.

Though he uses MacIntyre's work on ethics to elucidate his work on *Coordinated Management of Meaning Theory*, Vernon E. Cronen (1991) critiques MacIntyre's limiting of his work on traditions to that of Western traditions. "The effect of this was to lose sight of the fact that Western traditions are held together by diverse and widely known set of cultural practices. [. . .] By losing track of the broader conception, culture, MacIntyre failed to see the diversity of resources by which one tradition may encounter another" (p. 33). MacIntyre responded to his critiques in the preface of the second edition of *A Short History of Ethics*, published in 1997, by acknowledging some of the philosophers he did not include in the first edition, as well as suggesting that his work was the "short" history of Western ethics and, therefore, the book should be read as such (pp. vii-xix).

There are, indeed, modern-day scholars writing on universal ethics and third world countries, all of which are valid and important. Gerald A. Larue (1993) offers an insightful explanation of ethics in ancient Mesopotamia and suggests that once writing was developed stories were written about

> heroes who exemplified virtues most admired, legal codes that defined acceptable and non-acceptable conduct and instructional formulations, all of which inform us about the nature of ethics as it first developed into something sufficiently explicit to be the subject of reflection and discussion. [. . .] Western ethics has its roots in these ancient approaches to the problems of regulating a settled society. (p. 29)

Celebrity advocacy is hero driven. American society looks to our sports heroes, as with the National Football League supporting the United Way in their work to raise money or gain support for community groups. Or the Olympian who is a spokesperson for a children's cause. We applaud these people who are top in their fields, who have exemplified courage, tenacity, and vigor to achieve their goal. Sometimes we put media celebrities in the same categories as sports heroes.

Another view from a non-Western tradition explained by Purusottama Bilimoria (1993), discusses Indian ethics:

> In India it was recognized that ethics is the "soul" of the complex spiritual and moral aspirations of the people, co-mingled with social and political structures forged over a vast period of time. And this is a recurrent leitmotif in the culture's profuse wisdom literature, legends, epics, liturgical texts, legal and political treaties. (p. 43)

Therefore, it is not that these important societies are being ignored, but rather, this work notes that the West does not have the sole key that unlocked the doors to the house of ethics. An interesting fact in Bilimoria's explanation is that ethics can be found in the small narratives of literature as well as legal documents, texts that identify both implicitly and explicitly the communication that occurred within a culture regarding the overarching agreements found within an ethical community. However, to look at American political discourse, MacIntyre's work can assist us in thinking in terms of Western philosophy, as described and expanded upon in *A Short History of Ethics*, as well as *After Virtue*.

Ethics has a long history of people engaging questions as to what is the appropriate decision, what ought to be done (Jensen, 1991), and how the search should be conducted for the morally and ethically correct answer (Andersen, 1991). These central questions propel the writing of what is considered the hallmark of ethical theory, Aristotle's *Nichomachean Ethics*, through to the modern-day listing of Henry Sidgwick's (1907/1981) engagement of the contemporary conversation of ethics in his *The Methods of Ethics*. These ethical questions become communication action metaphors in communication ethics, guiding the way for a discussion of the practical maneuvers toward, and consequences for, communication ethics. Therefore, ethics are distinguished from communication ethics in an effort to enlighten discussion around the actions of ethics woven throughout our communicative efforts during engagement with other community members (civil, political, religious, familial societies).

Alasdair MacIntyre's *After Virtue* (1981/1984), a scholarly exposition that followed the first (1966) edition of *A Short History of Ethics* by 25 years, explained his vision of the danger of ignoring praxis and the connection between theory and action, and suggests the Enlightenment was a failed project, and that we have lost our teleological compass. Therefore, we find competing narratives in postmodernity, each having its own compass. MacIntyre (1981/1984) explains that "emotivism," a practical and philosophical plight, is used to explain decision making centered on one's "preference, expressions of attitude or feeling, insofar as they are moral or evaluative in character" (p. 12). Emotivism turns us away from thoughtful, grounded, knowing action. Therefore, examining practical applications of ethics is crucial for contemporary students.

Robert Bellah, Richard Madsen, William M. Sullivan, Ann

Swidler, and Steven M. Tipton (1985) engaged in such a work in
Habits of the Heart, an elongated sociological explanation of what
happens "after virtue" (p. xii). Bellah et al. discuss problems that
occur when the focus is on individuals themselves, thus limiting us
in formation of bonded communities. Bellah discusses praxis of human community and how, in terms of emotivism, individualism is
problematic.

In terms of gestalt theory, offering a basis by which to understand our own current-day history in terms of what came before and
the actions that follow (backgrounding and foregrounding), would
be beneficial for logically defining why decisions were made as well
as analyzing implications of those decisions. Identifying rhetorical
interruptions may assist us with recognizing current-day struggles
in our own postmodern lives.

Rhetorical Interruptions

Communicative disparity that characterizes fluctuations from
one time to the other–the movement from ancient Greece to the
Christianity of the Middle Ages, to the Enlightenment, to Modernity, and then to postmodernity–can be viewed as "rhetorical interruptions" (Hyde, 2001, p. 78). Michael Hyde describes and expands
on Martin Heidegger's notion of "historical call," and the changes
that occur in our lives because of this call from one person to another. A sense of transformation occurs when one realizes that things
are not as they once were. Springsteen's lyrics are full of that announcement, of the notion that we are not the America we used to
be. Springsteen questioned the Iraq War in his 2005 album *Devils
and Dust* and now with his new release, *Magic*, he explores the notion that "we will be the last to die for our mistake," an echo of John
Kerry's testimony on Vietnam (Du Lac, 2007).

Hyde (2001) suggests "that the call of conscience is itself a rhetorical interruption" (p. 78). Discussing the interruptions and the
outcome on human communication and the ethical implications of
choice making will assist the student of ethics in determining what
worked in the past and, potentially, how to make decisions in the
future. Therefore, this work seeks to understand history through
the contemporary significance of ideas, figures, and events. Time
lies not only behind, but also beside and in front of us. *Rolling Stone*
critic David Fricke (2004a) suggested in his review of *Devils and
Dust*, "But many of Springsteen's best songs, going back to 'Born

to Run,' are about the salvation just out of reach, around the next curve and over the next hill–and what it takes to get there." Springsteen's music is about coming alive in the moment, when there is a chance for redemption. According to his decision to work to defeat the incumbent president, it was time for a change and he had to take the chance.

Explaining the importance of the historical moment and how rhetorical interruptions allow those moments to come alive, Ronald C. Arnett (2005) suggests that the moment speak to those listening:

> It is a moment that calls clearly. Communication does not rest with us alone; the historical moment speaks. It is our response that furthers the conversation. History is marked by public points of memory. Awareness of the significance of a given historical moment begins with a rhetorical interruption, calling us from the routine of everyday life into response, into what both Bonhoeffer and Levinas would call responsibility. (p. 5)

The historical moment spoke to those who engaged in celebrity advocacy during the Vote for Change tour. Because Bruce Springsteen had never been partisan in his politics before the 2004 presidential election, people questioned his reasoning for his absolute support in defeating President George W. Bush. It was a rhetorical interruption that called to him and he could not pass up the opportunity.

Celebrity Advocacy: Answering the Rhetorical Interruption

We are accustomed to seeing sports stars endorse athletic equipment, sports drinks, and clothing, and many in the target audience react by purchasing the endorsed product. We are familiar with watching famous models wear the newest clothing, and we want to buy those very clothes. Celebrities continue to influence decision making down to the minutest levels of personal buying habits/patterns. Why, then are we afraid to allow a celebrity to endorse a political candidate?

As mentioned, in October 2007 Springsteen released his newest collaboration with the E-Street Band, his musical companions of 30 years. *Magic* may be considered Springsteen's most political album to date. A.O. Scott (2007) of the *New York Times* interviewed Springsteen a week before the release of *Magic* and explained the context in which Springsteen wrote the new material:

> And while the songs on "Magic" characteristically avoid explicit topical references, there is no mistaking that the source of the unease is, to a great extent, political. The title track, Mr. Springsteen explained, is about the manufacture of illusion, about the Bush administration's stated commitment to creating its own reality. "This is a record about self-subversion," he told me, about the way the country has sabotaged and corrupted its ideals and traditions. And in its own way the album itself is deliberately self-subverting, troubling its smooth, pleasing surfaces with the blunt acknowledgment of some rough, unpleasant facts. (2007)

The first leg of the fall 2007 Magic tour sold out in less than one hour in a dozen U.S. cities. Springsteen concert tickets sold out even more quickly for his European dates in 2007-2008. There are at least 20,000 people in each of these cities who don't mind hearing the political lyricist, and are, in fact, willing to spend a hundred dollars to hear it espoused!

Standing in the beginning of the twenty-first century, we can see changes. A rhetorical shift has occurred; things are no longer what they used to be in America. Educating the public about the value of narrative-driven communication, communication that is embedded in a faithful narrative, that has fidelity (Makau, 1991) and coherence (Fisher, 1984) is important for postmodern times in general, and more specifically, for the decision-making process that comes out of rhetorical interruptions. Fidelity involves promise keeping, and coherence involves logic and consistency in decision making.

Decisions, such as voting for the president of the United States, carry great weight for all Americans. Critics will contend that something this important should not be influenced by popular culture. But guess what? Popular culture invades everything we do in this postmodern moment. "And what defines the heart and soul of America, as much as the fight over the war in Iraq or health care reform, is why popular culture has become so much a part of Campaign 2004" (Raasch, 2004) and future campaigns yet to arrive. Technology has ensured the West that information can be carried to our ear, our computer, our doorstep faster than ever imagined possible. We will be influenced by more than teachers, by more than religious leaders, by more than family.

As consumers of this popular culture, whether by payment, turning the button on, or by osmosis, we need to be educated and aware of where the persuader stands. We should attempt to understand where his or her statements come from and on what ground the speaker stands? If embedded in a narrative, the communicative influence should be apparent and coherent.

Celebrity advocates have a place in our society, but it is incumbent on the audience to determine whether they give credence to the message or not, and further if they are persuaded to act. Bruce Springsteen, Bono, Michael J. Fox–they are all names. But, do their words, their calls to action, ßtheir arguments stand the test of veracity? As consumers, we must be educated in the debate, and as with anyone who attempts to persuade us, we are prepared to attend to the information, and then make an informed decision to act or not.

Notes

1   The Dixie Chicks, a Grammy award winning female country/pop band, dealt with a pop culture battle of both fans and non-fans alike when, during a concert in 2003, lead singer, Natalie Maines suggested that they were embarrassed that President Bush was from Texas. In the aftermath of this announcement, the group's music was banned from some radio stations, and record sales plummeted.

They subsequently entitled a documentary about their comeback after that public outcry "Shut Up and Sing" because they would hear that shouted from the audience. The group rebounded from the public ostracizing and won a Grammy Award for their album Not Ready to Make Nice.

2   In this instance, stumped indicates "supported" as a candidate. A stump speech is an 18th century way of saying campaign speech, because men used to stand on tree stumps to stand above the crowd to offer a political agenda/platform prior to the days of formal stage settings.

3   Actor Courteney Cox, famed for her many years on the phenomenally successful sitcom *Friends,* was known ten years earlier as a young "fan" who was chosen to be pulled out of an audience to dance in a music video with Bruce Springsteen during "Dancing in the Dark." The casual music fan would have these recollections about Springsteen's music, and understand him to be a member of pop culture, but not necessarily a man who understood politics enough to campaign for a presidential candidate.

References

2004 Election Exit Poll Results. (n.d.). Retrieved September 10, 2007, from http://www.beliefnet.com/story/155/story_15546_1.html

Andersen, Kenneth E. (1991). A history of communication ethics. In K. J. Greenberg (Ed.), *Conversations on communication ethics* (pp. 3-20). Norwood, NJ: Ablex.

Aristotle. (1998). *The Nicomachean ethics.* (D. Ross, Rev. J. L. Ackrill & J. O. Urmson, Trans.). Oxford: Oxford University Press.

Arnett, R. C. (2005). *Dialogic confession: Bonhoeffer's rhetoric of responsibility.* Carbondale: Southern Illinois University Press.

Bellah, R. N., Madsen, R., Sullivan, W. M., Swidler, A., & Tipton, S. M. (1985). *Habits of the heart.* Berkeley: University of California Press.

Bilimoria, P. (1993). Indian ethics. In P. Singer (Ed.), *Blackwell companions to philosophy: A companion to ethics* (pp. 43-57). Oxford: Blackwell.

Carpenter, M. (2004, September 26). Arts & politics: Stars of every stripe stump for their candidate. *Pittsburgh Post-Gazette.* Retrieved October 1, 2004, from www.pittsburghpostgazette.com/pg/pp/04270/384297.stm

Cronen, V. E. (1991). Coordinated management of meaning theory and postenlightenment ethics. In K. J. Greenberg (Ed.), *Conversations on communication ethics* (pp. 21-53). Norwood, NJ: Ablex.

Du Lac, J. F. (2007, October 2). Springsteen's magic casts a darker spell. *Washington Post,* p. C01.

Fisher, W. R. (1984). Narration as a human communication paradigm: The case of public moral argument. *Communication Monographs, 51* (1), 1-22.

Fox, M. J. (2002). *Lucky man.* New York: Hyperion.

Fricke, D. (2004a, January 1). Bruce Springsteen: Devils and dust. *Rolling Stone.* Retrieved September 20, 2007, from http://www.rollingstone.com.reviews/album/7237604/review/7263906?utm_source=Rhapsody&utm medium=CDreview

———. (2004b, September 2). Taking it to the streets. *Rolling Stone, 956,* 37-38.

Gadamer, H. G. (2002). *Truth and method.* New York: Continuum.

Hyde, M. J. (2001). *The call of conscience.* Columbia: University of South Carolina Press.

Jensen, J. V. (1991). Foreword. In K. J. Greenberg (Ed.), *Conversations on communication ethics* (pp. x-xiii). Norwood, NJ: Ablex.

Knickmeyer, E. (2006, November 6). Hussein sentenced to death by hanging. *Washington Post Foreign Service.* p. A01. Retrieved October 2, 2007,from http://www.washingtonpost.com/wp-dyn/content/article/2006/11/05/AR2006110500135.html.

Larue, G. A. (1993). Ancient ethics. In P. Singer (Ed.), *Blackwell companions to philosophy: A companion to ethics* (pp. 29-40). Oxford: Blackwell.

MacIntyre, A. (1981/1984). *After virtue.* 2nd ed. Notre Dame, IN: University of Notre Dame Press.

———. (1998). *A short history of ethics: A history of the moral philosophy from the Homeric age to the twentieth century.* Notre Dame, IN: University of Notre Dame Press.

Makau, J. M. (1991). The principles of fidelity and veracity: Guidelines for ethical communication. In K. J. Greenberg (Ed.), *Conversations on communication ethics* (pp. 111-120). Norwood, NJ: Ablex.

Margolis, J. (2004, August 17). Box-office campaigns. *New York Times,* p. A21.

Marsh, D. (2006). *Bruce Springsteen on tour* 1968-2005. New York: Bloomsbury USA.

Montgomery, D. (2006, October 25). Rush Limbaugh on the offensive against and with Michael J. Fox. *Washington Post.com.* Retrieved November 1, 2006, from http://www.washingtonpost.com/wpdyn/content/article/2006/10/24/AR200610 2400691_pf.html

National commission on terrorist attacks upon the United States. (2004) 10.2: *Planning for war*. Retrieved September 20, 2004, from http://www.9-11commission.gov/report/911Report_Ch10.htm

Ohio election results 2004. (2004, November 24). *WashingtonPost.com*. Retrieved October 4, 2007, from http://www.washingtonpost.com/wp-srv/elections/2004/oh/

Raasch, C. (2004). Pop culture saturates presidential campaign. *USA Today*. Retrieved May 31, 2007, from http://www.usatoday.com/news/politicselections/nation/president/2004-10-26-pop-culture-races_x.htm

Saddam Hussein arrested in Iraq. (2003, December 14). *BBC NEWS*. Retrieved September 10, 2007, from http://news.bbc.co.uk/2/hi/middle_east/3317429.stm

Scott, A.O. (2007, September 30). In love with pop, uneasy with the world. *New York Times*. Retrieved October 1, 2007, from http://www.nytimes.com/2007/09/30/arts/music/30scot.html?pagewanted=print

Seccombe, M. (2007, August). Michael J. Fox paces through life of writing. Vineyard Press. Michael J. Fox Foundation. Retrieved October 2, 2007, from http://www.michaeljfox.org/newsEvents_michaelInTheNews_article.cfm?ID=35

Sidgwick, H. (1907/1981). *The methods of ethics,* 7th ed. Foreword by John Rawls. Indianapolis: Hackett.

Soeder, J. (2005). Analysis: Rocker Bono parlays fame into advocacy for the desperate. *The Plain Dealer*. Retrieved March 12, 2007 from Lexisnexis database.

Weinstein, J. R. (2003). *On MacIntyre*. Toronto: Thomson Wadsworth.

Chapter 3

Ethical Dialogue in the Classroom

Reverend John Amankwah

The classroom is like a playground where both the teacher and students engage each other in an exchange that gradually reaches a crescendo of insightful appreciation of knowledge. The play moves through a communicative process of exploration evolving experiences of entry into a dialectical tension, of exiting, and learning from each other. It facilitates the symbolic formation of learning from each of the participants, and the experiential outcome is directed toward the inducement of human knowing. This symbolic formation through dialogic experience in the classroom points to dialogue as a reflective questioning and systemic inquiry through which the dialectical tensions inherent in the pursuit of knowledge are positioned as both the means of analysis and the means of intervention (Kellett & Dalton, 2001).

Dialogue thus is not simply a mere speech or a mere interaction between people, but rather the dynamics permeating the dialogic encounter demonstrate a qualitative encounter of people who are serious to meet each other on a "narrow ridge" (Buber, 1967, p. 55). It is the "between" (Buber, 1967, p. 24) which, Buber claims, defines the willingness of the participants in the conversation and their orientation toward one another in a given historical moment. The historicality of the given moment in the classroom driven by the emergence of new ideas may also promote a completely different nuance in the interaction that can result in bringing the dialogists–teacher and students-closer together.

Philosophical Understanding of Dialogue

Generally, in our day-to-day interactive communication, dialogue is assumed to be simply back and forth conversation that people engage in. However, this vernacular understanding misses the nuance of philosophical approaches to dialogue from whence the term in common usage sprang. Important to dialogue are the emerging processes that direct the encounter and embed the parties in the dialogic environment to create a common focus with diverse perspectives. In the words of Martin Buber, dialogue is the "between on the extremes on the narrow ridge" (Buber, 1998, pp. iii-ix). To Buber, the dialogue on the narrow ridge evokes a crisis that gradually draws the interactants together in their search for mutual understanding, respect for each other's opinion, and confirmation and disconfirmation of one another (Anderson, Cissna & Arnett, 1994).

In the dialogue, the interactants search for meanings produced in the "saying" (Cohen, 1998; Levinas, 1983) because, within the interactive process, a search for meaning is vigorously pursued. For Buber, this search is driven by a new dialogical thinking situated within a panoramic horizon of philosophy in which the Thou is not a mere participant but is encountered within a space in which each of the partners assures the dignity of the other "as that of a Thou addressed to God" (Anderson, Cissna, Buber & Rogers, 1997, pp. 315-316). This new dialogical thought explains some of the dynamic processes that have emerged in interpersonal communication, and it exemplifies the authenticity of the mutuality of human beings.

Buber has influenced the field of dialogue through his reflection on the nature of the human person and his understanding of the other. His research has underscored the significance of human relationships in communities, which he calls "Interhuman" (Buber 1998). His work placed dialogue at the center of human interaction in which the Thou brings closer to the subject the historical consciousness of the moment. In the same vein, within the Gadamarian tradition, the interaction between people produces meanings rather than being reproduced by recipients individually, and the process is a collaborative kind (Gadamer, 1976). Increasing numbers of communication scholars cite Martin Buber, Hans-Georg Gadamer, Mikhail Bakhtin, and other authoritative voices in the field as sources to extend current work on dialogue. Their efforts have shed light on the concept of dialogue not only as an exchange of insights, perceptions, and ideas but also as a process of defining who we are in our interactive process.

In 1993, Klaus Krippendorff argued against "message-driven" explanation of communication, especially for the field of dialogue. Since then, numerous communication theories relevant to dialogue have emerged, including the theory of language and mind (Rommetveit, 1992) Gadamer's notion of the "word," "work," and "historicality" (Gadamer, 1989, 1960[1]), and the idea of Dialogism (Bakhtin, 1986). These and subsequent theories further helped to develop a turn toward the praxis nature of dialogue. David Berlo (1960) helped to free the notion of dialogue from its restraints as an unchanging communicative action by conceptualizing dialogue as a process, an active process that flows among persons, context, and topic. Dean Barnlund (1970) also recognized that communication is a complex process that comprises cross-linking sociocultural and psychological influences, illumining interaction with demonstrable and hidden meaning.

During this gradual development of the notion of dialogue in the 1970s and 1980s, much of the scholarly work focused on the assumptions of dialogue in the college and university campuses. The research was designed to emphasize the significance of dialogic interactions between professors and their students and the relationships on the campuses (Brown & Van Riper, 1973; Friedman, 1974). In short, much of the scholarly work was understood as part of the multivocal human activity among professors and students. Thus, the process changed from a univocal activity of the professor to a multivocal human activity involving students and the professor in the classroom. The underlying reason was to turn the learning experience in the classroom as involving both the students and the professor because, during a classroom interaction, both the students and the professor engage in a learning process through back-and-forthness of questioning and explaining, guided by a sense of ethics that evolves from mutual understanding and respect.

Dialoguing in the Classroom

Dialogue in the classroom leads to a continual process whereby those involved in the act of conversation listen to each other and question one another. The emerging process takes a different form of back-and-forthness processual stream of discourse that evolves uncertainties and clarifications through immediate interpretive action that keeps the conversation going. In her book *The Courage to Teach*, Parker J. Palmer (1998) notes that teaching as a field is a "truly human activity" that emerges from one's inwardness for better or for worse. As a human activity, the teaching profession is propelled by a selfless process of availability and a constant renunciation of our self-interests. The reason for this selflessness is the

multivocal nature of the activity in which teachers engage themselves and the inherent entanglements we encounter every day in
the classroom. The entanglements become a source of dialectics, as
educators experience competing multivocal expressions from those
taught. Palmer (1998) offers three sources of these tangles, namely:

- The subjects taught are as large and as complex as life
- The students taught are larger than life and even more
  complex
- Teaching, like any human activity, emerges from one's inwardness, for better or for worse. (p. 2)

According to Palmer (1998), because students are larger than
and as complex as life, it is always difficult to gain a full understanding of who they are and this makes educators' knowledge of
these students flawed and partial. The situation therefore drives
educators to intensify teaching skills and research. In most cases,
educators find themselves being eluded by our efforts. Second, to be
able to understand students and wisely go along with them, Palmer
(1998) notes that it "demands the fusion of Freud and Solomon" (p.
2). Third, the entanglements experienced in the classroom are at
times indicative of the teacher's own inner convolutions. Educators
feel inadequate at times and see themselves in the mirror of the
soul, and those who are bold enough to see themselves in the mirror of the soul do gain self-confidence because, in confronting themselves, they pull themselves together and move on.

Recently, after an uncomfortable incident in one of my classes, I
came away from the classroom depressed, feeling sorry for myself,
and the depression turned into anger. I went to my office, sat down,
and said to myself, "There is no point being angry. Let me call the
student to the office and initiate a dialogue with her." Immediately,
I sent an e-mail to the student asking her to come over to my office the next day so that we could talk about the incident that took
place in the classroom. I checked my e-mail in the evening to find
out whether she responded. Yes, she did but with an emphatic no!
I found myself hitting the wall. How do I go in tomorrow and teach
the class? I went home that day feeling very depressed and sad. This
experience is not pertinent to me alone, I am sure. It is likely that
many professors have had the same experience. However, the question is, what does a teacher do in such an aggravating situation?

Ethical dialogue demands an equal acceptance of opinions, and it further extends the interaction to the extremes of recognizing the other in the interaction as equal, and therefore to be accorded with the deserved dignity. And for the sake of "in defense of Public Speaking," the teaching profession points us in the direction that opinions expressed by students in the classroom be deemed acceptable with utmost patience and respect. Feelings of inadequacy are a sign of weakness in the class, as Palmer noted, and therefore, the teacher is called on to pick up the bits and pieces and move along with the students. The dialectics that emerge in the teaching process is part and parcel of the profession because it always evolves new horizons and possibilities.

Dialectical Dialogue in the Classroom

The term "dialogism" characterizes Bakhtin's (1986) view and was first applied by Holquist in his translation of Bakhtin's work (p. 75). In the Bakhtinian tradition, dialogism embodies the cacophony of a conversational reverberational process that considers the indeterminate nature of conversation. Bakhtin's application of the term dialogism separates him from the Hegelian-Marxian notion of dialectics that is seen by him as an overly simplistic conception of contradiction that smothers lived experience. Accordingly, Bakhtin understands such contradiction as basically resting on a monologic strand in the single consciousness of synthesis that evolves from the struggle of thesis against antithesis. Bakhtin uses the term "dialogue" in several interrelated senses—everyday dialogue, actual dialogue, and real-life dialogue to refer to the everyday conversation in which two people speak with one another on different topics freely and without compulsion for whatever length of time. He calls this kind of everyday conversation "the simplest and most classic form of speech communication" (Bakhtin, 1986, p. 147).

However, Bakhtin notes that dialogue can also be understood in the context of less immediate encounters, for instance, published papers by a number of authors on a particular topic. In this sphere of dialogue, one is not only dealing with physical encounter but also with the incorporation of one's utterance in another's view expressed in writing or speech. He summarizes his view on this impersonal encounter by stating that "in any utterance there is a link in the chain of speech communication, which cannot be broken off from the preceding links because the utterance is also related to subsequent links in the chain of speech communication" (Bakhtin, 1986, p. 147). Within this criticism of the Hegelian-Marxian notion of thesis-antithesis-synthesis, Bakhtin notes that it would be wrong to conceive of dialectics as a single continuum with a determinate character because ordinarily, in everyday conversation, participants do not engage in a formal format by stating their thesis, antithesis, and then their conclusion. Instead, the centripetal and centrifugal elements that permeate the conversational utterances are "always constituted in the immediate context, thereby affording the voices concrete complexity and fluidity" (Bakhtin, 1996, pp. 30-32). Bakhtin's argument here connects well with the Buberian notion of the crisis of the "between" in which participants engage each other in conversation in the historical moment. The outcome of such dialogic engagement is without certainty. Rather, each participant in the conversation endeavors to participate in the dialogic interaction with mutual and respectful presence to search and reach new understandings.

The inherent task in the teaching profession reflects the intense dialectics pointed out by Bakhtinian and Buberian sense of dialectics that is driven by a sense of a multivocal participation. Through such dialectics, the teacher finds voice among the many competing voices of the students' stories that are embedded, in many cases, in postmodern metanarratives inherent in the historical moment. The tasks and the challenges the teacher faces are propelled by constant attempts to search and discover his/her voice within the often concatenating and polyphonic world of students.

Further, a Bakhtinian notion of dialectics (1929a) accepts the existence of inevitability inherent in the idea of dialogism. He notes that this inevitability within dialogism should be understood as a way of engaging the other in an open conversation so that the evolution of variety of issues can lead participants to search for a consensus ground. Primarily, what Bakhtin (1929a; 1984) seeks to explain is that our relational dialectics have been "gradually and slowly wrought out of" (pp. 290-293) the foundational and imagined dialogues because of the postmodernist idea of metanarratives. However, although he does not dismiss the postmodernist's stance of seeing all the "mishmash" in social life, he underscores the significance of the postmodernist interplay of multivocal mishmash that is filled with a sense of centripetal and centrifugal voices. In short, for Bakhtin, life by its very nature is dialogic. To live means to participate in dialogue: to ask questions, to heed, to respond, to agree, and so forth. In this dialogue, a person participates wholly and through-out his whole life: with his eyes, lips, hands, soul, spirit, with his whole body, and deeds. He invests his entire self in discourse, and this discourse enters into the dialogic fabric of human life, into the world symposium (Bakhtin, 1984). This notion reveals the difficulty the teacher experiences with the rough currents of postmodernism that often assumes speech enshrouded in the cloak of "in defense of Public Speaking."

Thus, the teacher is encouraged to admit other views rather than maintain what Stewart (1991) calls a "monadic, processual stream of rationality," which is contrary to the understanding of humans as "beings-in-relation" (p. 361) and which really involves dialecti-cal voices. All these different views demonstrate that dialogue is an enactment of communication and admits the constant flux of dialec-tics. These dialectics turn the teaching profession inside out from a monologue that commands, objectifies, and demands a subdued voice in the relational encounter by attenuating the dialectic flux to open other avenues for the participants. The enactment of dialec-tic voices also encourages the dialogic process to search for ethical ground of the between. The type of dialectics that Bakhtin talks about is not reduced to simple and mechanistic dialectics experi-enced in relationships like openness versus closedness, autonomy versus connection, certainty versus novelty, but dialectics necessary for any open conversation (Baxter & Montgomery, 1996).

Both Bakhtin and Stewart do agree that dialectic contradictions must be understood in terms of "complex overlapping, domains of centrifugal forces juxtaposed with centripetal forces" (Baxter & Montgomery, 1996, pp. 42-44). Further, the authors point out that in every relationship, there is a dynamic opposing association that promotes an ongoing conversation and consequently permit change. In addition, their observation is highlighted by the notion that so-cial interactions always admit polyphones that involve multiple, valid voices that represent different perspectives, no matter what the issue is.[2] The views of the authors are significant because ethical dialogue in the classroom invites cooperation of diverse and varied voices to keep the process going.

Ethical Dialogue

Ethical dialogue admits various complexities of opinions inher-ent in any dialogue and it seeks to depart from monologue that rests on the assumption of "sameness" (Baxter & Montgomery, 1996, p. 45). Ethical dialogue in the classroom seeks to involve the admission of multiplicity of competing voices. The elements in these competing voices propel the dynamics of the ongoing conversation, that is, to respond to each other's opinions and further embark on an exploratory journey to search for mutual consensus. The monologic unidirectional consistency that at times characterizes the teaching profession can often constitute a fixation with the teacher as the center of analysis to the neglect of the student. Such characterization is also comparable to the Archimedean and Cartesian understanding of the human person as the sole monadic processual stream of being. In fact, Bakhtin (1929b) emphasizes that a unidirectional stance in dialogue reduces the other to "merely an object of consciousness, and not another consciousness" whose involvement "could change everything in the world of my consciousness" (p. 293). We learn a great deal of lessons from our students when we critically listen and become part of their often mishmash multivocal expressions. By emphasizing the significance of multivocal inclusion within a dialogic encounter, Bakhtin points us to an ethical dialogue that calls for an inclusive and interactive process necessary for the classroom experience.

The application of the metaphor of "healing" is an apt phrase in this context. The teacher is called to bring healing to the student. The material prepared to elucidate the confused field of knowledge of the student can be directed toward the restoration of sight to the student, release him from the captivity of ignorance and confusion, and embed him/her in the synthesis of academic freedom. Further, this mission can be contextualized within the biblical notion of announcing the Good News to the poor and proclaiming the year of favor as enunciated in Isaiah 62 (New American Catholic Bible). These activities are not achieved through a unidirectional mode of dialogue in the classroom. Rather, the activities lead both the teacher and the students to a search that permits vocal inclusiveness in the ongoing academic dialogue in the classroom.

Ethical dialogue in the classroom also recognizes the frictions inherent in the struggle to uncover the finiteness of knowledge in the world of the students' existence. The task to be accomplished in the teaching profession is driven toward the reality of coexistence that challenges "unsubstantiated optimism and utopianism" (Arnett, 1997, p. 31) in the world of students because it is through the messiness of life that meaning is given to human experience. This reality of coexistence in the classroom portrays an ironic view of the teaching profession and it reveals the "unity of contraries" embedded in the teacher-student relationship.

Martin Buber (1966) offers a communicative view that focuses on the "unity of contraries" and he frames for us a communication ethic that rests on the dialectical nature of life whether in the classroom, at home, or in the marketplace. On one hand, the ethical dimension embedded in the notion of "unity of contraries" is capable of upholding the moral claims of the academy by revealing the significance of "human togetherness" while on the other hand concentrating on a political realism that is capable of acknowledging the inclusive and exclusive nature of human community. The teaching profession possesses this symbolic nature, and so it makes sense to bring to bear in the teacher-student relationship the academic realism of acknowledging the essence of the profession as a dialogic and nurturing experience that heals and restores both the teacher and the students to academic holism.

It is also important in acknowledging the realism of a sense of community within the context of the teacher-student relationship to recognize that those who are entrusted to teachers to educate (that is, to lead out–*educere*) come to the educator with diverse historical experiences, which in many cases are flavored with youthful exuberance. The three central metaphors of the agrarian era, the industrial era, and the postmodern or information era, as employed by Arnett and Arneson (1999), are contextually significant because they inform us of how our sense of community as a field of relations has changed. The authors note that communities in the agrarian era had a sense of place, a locale. The metaphor of place ties the members of the community to the land (Brueggemann, 1977; Arnett & Arneson, 1999), where their myths, stories, and narratives grounded them in their historical, traditional, and cultural beliefs. These elements gave them a sense of belongingness. In the same vein, the students leave home and come to an institution where they have to learn to live with strangers. It points to the industrial era. The transition from the locale that gave them a sense of belongingness into the industrial period disintegrated the agrarian community and sent members off to far distant lands into the urban areas, displacing the homeland and their sense of belongingness with a sense of self. In the life of the student, the reality of myth, story, and narrative forged with parents and friends in their towns and villages get lost and give way to a sense of emotivism (actions based on feelings) because of loss of security. The institutional compound for the student becomes a strange place and often brings about nostalgic emotivism.

The information era, as Arnett and Arneson point out, characterizes our present age, in which structures of metanarrative have declined and, in place of narrative, the primary focus of attention is directed toward the self with an eventual culmination into an egoistic narcissism. I remember during one of my classes, a student challenged another student for giving her persuasive speech on Dafur in Sudan, North Africa. During the questioning and response period, the student told the speaker that she could not understand the reason for preparing her speech on a country so far away from home. "I think U.S. should not give help to any country. For me, I am egoistic and we should all remain egoistic," said the critical student. As Arnett and Arneson explain, although the search for wisdom in all three periods (agrarian, industrial, and informational) took different turns with different perspectives, there is still the need to assist the postmodern era with dialogically informed stories that we tell one another. Teachers have the burden of inculcating this sense of "stories" into students to enhance their worldview and help them appreciate the significance of narratives in the postmodern era. Further, the authors note that in working to bring dialogue in an era of postmodern decline of metanarrative, educators' efforts must be guided by a sense of the historical moment that invites dialogic civility.

Teachers should be encouraged to consider the teaching profession as an invitation to assist in creating a community that communicates this sense of place, self, and the sharing of the stories emerging from our ethical sense of dialogue. In order that these stories may carry meaning for the students and create a sense of community of relations, the stories must be dialogically informed. The classroom experience will then be a departure from the old model of teaching when students were constantly informed in a univocal communicative formula that hardly offered them any chance of telling their own stories for comparison and thus contribute to the ongoing story. In the context of a univocal communicative formula, students often lose their chance to engage in serious ethical dialogic conversation. John Shotter (1993) reminds us that a monologic practice only promotes "deafness to the interplay of voices" (p. 62) because no other voices are included.

Formation of Teacher and Students in Ethical Dialogue

Further, the task for the teacher is to nurture and nourish the students entrusted to him/her and recognize that there are always dialectical elements in classroom relations. Though these dialectical tensions often lead to unsurpassable tensions, the inevitabilities should not lead to ignoring some students through silence or neglect. Such response stands contrary to the encouragement that is to characterize the attitude of teachers. In fact, the teacher is reminded to recall his/her experiences with other professors who shaped and strengthened his/her views and in the same vein come to terms with Jesus' words to Peter in Luke 22:32-33: "Simon, I have prayed for you that your faith may not fail, and once you have recovered, you in turn must strengthen your brothers" (New American Catholic Bible). This idea of encouragement through care is what gives the teacher-student relationship and fosters a sense of hope that drives the relationship to focus on enhancing the worldviews of the students through ethical dialogue.

The teaching activity in the classroom is therefore directed to form a community that looks ahead with a sense of hope. The hope enables the members of the teaching community to grapple with the emerging difficulties and demands of everyday life. Further, the hope enables the teacher to depart from the often "oxymoronic tension" (Shotter, 1993, p. 32) inherent in the false notion of commonality, optimism, difference, and idealism. In fact, Paolo Freire (1970) reminds us that unless a story is supported by actions, it remains dead, and a story becomes worthy of participation when people live what is spoken. Words without the congruence of praxis, that is, words without experiential activities, only invite lives of lies and deception, not a community or dialogue between people. Freire (1970) thus argues that community is nourished by characters willing to tell a story that they attempt to live, simultaneously inviting others to continue to shape the story and the practical life of the community.

Martin Buber calls our attention to the unification and vivification of such community's life through the "unity of contraries" that admits different voices and opinions in ethical dialogue. He explains in a piece concerning the dialogue between Israel and the Arabs, "I do not make a basic distinction between what is right morally and what is right politically...One has to sacrifice temporary benefits for future existence" (Menders-Flohr, 1983, p. 266). Buber therefore recognizes that dialogue rests on allowing the other "to be" through the sacrifice of the self and especially when it concerns young men and women whose futures are entrusted to us. In this context, the students' community should be encouraged to nurture its beliefs in the sharing of their stories that permit mutual nourishment and support for growth into maturity with the academic narrative as a guiding principle. The onus does not rest only on the students but on both teacher and students.

Overall, it is important to emphasize that the paradigm of ethical dialogue in the classroom does not completely invalidate the practice of monologic dialogue in the history of the teaching profession. Rather, it takes into consideration the different aspects emerging from the different counterpoints. The permeating of countervailing voices, according to Baxter and Montgomery (1996), points to the fact that the emerging countervailing voices underscore the dualistic thinking necessary for dialogue because of the acknowledgment of simple expressions and static polarities anchored in a single dimensional voice. Often the characterization of dualistic dialogical practice has not been the stance of the teaching profession because of the hierarchical nature of the field exemplified in the binary opposites of knowledge versus ignorance, superior versus subordinate, adult versus youth that recalls the Aristotelian hierarchical nature of society.

Ethical dialogue in the classroom suggested by this work affirms the shift from the dualistic expressions in which one polarity overrides the others emanating from an objectification to interplay of all the opposing forces inherent in the dialectical nature of dialogue. Bakhtin's notion of dialogism with its relational elements is foundational to the paradigm of ethical dialogue in the classroom because it calls for an acceptance of the individual within relational dialectics that drive the ethical dialogue.

Conclusion: The "Messiness" of Ethical Dialogue in the Classroom

In light of these assumptions underlying the paradigm of ethical dialogue, the teacher is invited to appreciate and understand the multiple perspectives of communicative events within the teaching profession. Ethical dialogue in the classroom also involves situating the life of the students within the larger definition of life as an ongoing and undeterminable chain of events, always becoming, changing, and transforming itself and its environment although disallowing ossification of its vital fabric. The process is explicated by Baxter and Montgomery (1996): "There are no ideal goals, no ultimate endings, no elegant end states of balance. There is only an indeterminate flow, full of unforeseeable potential that is realized in interaction" (p. 47). The authors point to the messiness of dialogue that never emerges as a methodological process, but as a process that is in constant motion of evolution that is transforming itself in an unceasing swing, like a pendulum, through time and history.

The challenges educators face in the classroom point to the fact that teachers need to be vigilant in adapting methods of teaching to the prevailing situation. I remember another incident in the classroom when one of the students, in the middle of my teaching with PowerPoint presentation, stopped me in my tracks and said: "Can we work in our groups so that we participate fully in the class?" For a moment, I froze, then looked at my presentation, and said to the class: "Let me finish with this block of materials and you can work in groups." It is within this context that we have to understand this paradigm-ethical dialogue, because it points to and affirms the very existence of the teaching profession as involved in a "messier" activity that constantly calls for a kinosic attitude from the teacher and students to be there for the Other.

In the past, students have been silenced for criticizing the teacher but from a hindsight and especially in the context of "in defense of Public Speaking," the student has all the rights in the classroom to express his/her opinion within the boundaries of the institution's academic catalogue. In his most famous study of individual responses to organizational problems, *Exit, Voice, and Loyalty*, Albert O. Hirschman (1970) noted that the challenge of voice or open criticism of an organization is favored or accepted when (1) the dissenter has some degree of loyalty to the organization and (2) when the dissenter is perceived as being very loyal to merit a hearing.

> "Voice," as the articulation of a special interest requires a "blending of apparent contradictions" on one hand, and on the other, the dissenter must express his or her view so that organizational leaders [teachers] know and can be responsive to what the person or group [students] seeks. (p. 32)

Over the years, the teaching profession as transnational and bureaucratic academia has been successful in engaging in the management of multiple identities. The potency of the teaching profession resides in the hearts of both teachers and students; therefore, the metaphor of "power" as service should remain a guiding principle in the profession. As service, the profession calls for humility for the teacher to enter the classroom and listen to opinions that are contrary to the subject in process. Thus, the rhythms of our days and activities in the classroom depend largely on our willingness to perceive the course itself as a learning unit to exploit its entire unity. Using the imagery of the dance, according to Laura Nash (1982).

> The component parts of the semester can be likened to the parts of the dance performance, with the melody equal to the subject matter, the staging to the classroom, the mode to the distinctive academic style of the professor, and the dancers to those who participate in the class: students and teacher. Timing, pace, theme, and variatio---the formal components of a musical score and its performance–might well be applied to the semester.... Thus, the teacher is transformed from presenter of wisdom to dancer and composer, responsible for the music and for the way in which the dancers all work their art. (p. xii)

Teachers are part of the dancing team and are largely involved in the composition of the ethical dialogue that is directed toward shaping and reshaping both our minds and those of the students.

Notes

1. Hans-Georg Gadamer's work of *Truth and Method* (1960) was approximately 100 pages but made significant changes by adding the sections "The recovery of the fundamental Hermeneutic Problem" and "Analysis of historically effected consciousness." The transformation of the text from its original draft to the version published in 1960 reveals the long evolutionary period of about ten years that it took Gadamer to write *Truth and Method*. The work went through a second revision and translation by J. Weinsheimer and D.G. Marshall in 1989. For understanding of this section, see *Truth and Method* (second revision and translation) by J. Weinsheimer and D.G. Marshall in 1989, pp. 405-423.
2. Bakhtin's notion of dialogization becomes all the more significant in this work because it departs from the traditional notion of dialogue as a one-sided, univocal activity based solely on who possesses the knowledge and authority. Jurgen Habermas articulates similar views in his stance on Legitimation crisis in which he points out that consensus does not rest on who possesses knowledge but admits multiple voices for the sake of consensus. For a comprehensive reading, see Bakhtin, 1975.

References

Anderson, R., Cissna, K. N., & Arnett, R. C. (1994). *The reach of dialogue: Confirmation, voice, and community.* Cresskill, NJ: Hampton Press.

Anderson, R., Cissna, K. N., Buber, M., Rogers, C. (1997). *The Martin Buber-Carl Rogers dialogue.* Albany: State University of New York Press.

Arnett, R.C. (1997). Communication and community. In J. M. Makau & R. C. Arnett (Eds.), *Communication ethics in an age of diversity* (pp. 27-47). Urbana and Chicago: University of Illinois Press.

Arnett, R. C., & Arneson, P. (1999). *Dialogic civility in a cynical age: Community, hope and interpersonal relationship.* Albany: State University of New York Press.

Bakhtin, M. M. (1996). *Speech genres and other late essays by M. M. Bakhtin.* (C. Emerson, M. Holoquist, Vern. W. McGee, Eds.). Austin: University of Texas Press.

———. (1984, 1929a). The dialogic imagination: Four essays by M. M. Bakhtin. (M. Holoquist, Ed.). Austin: University of Texas Press.

———. (1984, 1929b). *Problems of Dostoevsky's poetics.* (C. Emerson, Ed. & Trans.). Minneapolis: University of Minnesota Press.

———. (1986). *Speech genres and other late essays.* Austin: University of Texas Press.

Barnlund, D. C. (1970). A transactional model of communication. In K. K. Sereno & C. D. Mortensen (Eds.), *Foundations of communication theory* (pp. 87-94). New York: Harper & Row.

Baxter, L. A. & Montgomery, B. M. (1996). *Relating: Dialogues and dialectics.* New York: Guilford Press.

Berlo, D. (1960). *The process of communication.* New York: Holt, Rinehart & Winston, Inc.

Brown, C. T. & Van Riper, C. (1973). *Communication in human relationships.* Skokie, IL: National Textbook.

Brueggemann, W. (1977). *The land: Place as gift, promise and challenge in biblical faith.* Philadelphia: Fortress Press.

Buber, M. (1966). *The way of response.* New York: Schocken Books.

———. (1967). *Between man and man.* Macmillan: New York.

———. (1998). *The knowledge of man: Selected essays.* Amherst, NY: Humanity Books.

Cohen, R. A. (1998). Introduction. In E. Levinas, (Ed.), *Otherwise than being or beyond essence* (pp. xvi-xlv). Pittsburgh, PA: Duquesne University Press.

Freire, P. (1970). *Pedagogy of the oppressed.* New York: Seabury Press.

Friedman, M. (1974). *Existential trust and the community of peace.* New York: E. P. Dutton.

Gadamer, H. G. (1989) *Truth and Method.* 2nd rev. edition. Trans. J. Weinsheimer and D. G. Marshall. New York: Crossroad.

———. (1976). *Philosophical hermeneutics.* (D. E. Linge, Ed. and Trans.). Berkeley: University of California Press.

Hirschman, A. O. (1970). *Exit, voice, and loyalty: Responses to decline in firms, organizations and states.* Cambridge, MA: Harvard University Press.

Kellett, P. M., & Dalton, D. G. (2001). Managing conflict in a negotiated world: A narrative approach to achieving dialogue and change. In R. Anderson, L. Baxter, & K. Cissna (Eds.), *Dialogue: Theorizing differences in communication studies.* Thousand Oaks, CA: Sage.

Levinas, E. (1983). Beyond intentionality. In A. Montefiore (Ed.), *Philosophy in France today* (pp. 100-115). Cambridge: Cambridge University Press.

Menders-Flohr, P. R. (Ed.). (1983). *A land of two peoples: Martin Buber on Jews and Arabs.* New York: Oxford University Press.

Nash, L. (1982). The rhythms of the semester. In M. Gullette (Ed.), *The art and craft of teaching.* Cambridge, MA: Harvard University Press.

Palmer, P. J. (1998). *The courage to teach: Exploring the inner landscape of a teacher's life.* San Francisco: Jossey-Bass.

Rommetveit, R. (1992). Outline of a dialogically based socio-cognitive approach to human cognition and communication. In A. H. Wold (Ed.), *The dialogic alternative: Towards a theory of language and mind* (pp. 19-44). Oslo: Scandinavian University.

Shotter, J. (1993). *Conversational realities.* London: Sage.

Stewart, J. (1991). A postmodern look at traditional communication postulates. *Western Journal of Speech Communication, 55* (4), 361.

Chapter 4

Narrative Identity and Public Memory in Morocco

Fadoua Loudiy

As historical beings, humans seek to make sense of their past that could inform them of the present and offer guidance to propel them into the future. This temporal quest for meaning is often a path that is fraught with many struggles and problems. Coming to terms with the past can be an agonizing process for individuals and groups alike, especially when their memory of the past is filled with violence, pain, and suffering. In other words, to have a claim on their present, nations need to know their past. National communities rely on rhetorical practices for the purpose of making sense of the past, constructing the present, and imagining the future. As Gerard Hauser (1999) explains, there exists a symbiotic relationship between a society's "self-production" and rhetoric (p. 114). This relationship is perhaps most evident in a nation's struggle to represent and remember its past and build its public memory, the vernacular form of history.

Although the construction of a nation's public memory is always ongoing, tragic events, such as the Holocaust in Germany, Apartheid in South Africa, and the "Years of Lead" in Morocco,[1] constitute "rhetorical interruptions" (Hyde, 2001, p. 78) that provide the opportunity for renewed self-understanding and self-definition. Even if they resist being totalized in official accounts, these events demand that they be remembered and inscribed in humanity's collective memory. Remembrance in this context becomes a hermeneutical effort, a creative act aimed at reconfiguring an impossible past, redefining a people's ethical aim, and reinvigorating citizens' political capacity to act. In Ricoeurian terms, it is "an indispensable way of giving a future to the past" (Kearney, 2004, p. 8).[2]

It is important to point out at this juncture that all communicative actions rely on some aspect of memory. As Carol Blair (2006) reminds us, memory has long been a subject of inquiry for students of communication, but she also notes that "Today we understand memory and its relationship to communication quite differently, particularly in recognizing that memory is not simply a mental operation that a person uses or that she or he can refine and improve" (p. 52). Whether we choose to call it collective, national, public, or communal, memory is a dynamic communicative practice with significant implications.[3] In other words, to remember an event is to choose to communicate something about the past, and such a choice necessarily impacts the way we engage the present and dream of the future. This temporal tension is helpful in thinking about the connection between narrative and identity.

Paul Ricoeur's approach to narrative hermeneutics privileges an understanding of the past as a rhetorical form, in an attempt to move beyond the psychoanalytical and therapeutic framework (healing, catharsis, and mourning) that is often implicit, if not explicit, in scholarly conversations. In addition to the individual psychological impact of the rhetorical act of testifying, narrating one's story has great ethico-political implications such as enabling action and restoring citizens' political capacity. Hence, Paul Ricoeur's philosophy of narrative identity, temporality, and ethics are particularly relevant to this discussion.

This chapter invites readers to think about the connection between public memory and narrative identity—as articulated by French phenomenologist Paul Ricoeur—and how the representation of a tragic and violent past shapes the present and the future of a nation. Informed by the particularity of the Moroccan case, the author seeks to gain insight into the inherently communicative and rhetorical nature of the practices involved in how a community chooses to remember its past. As the vernacular version of official history, public memory is a metaphor worthy of scholarship in communication studies precisely because the praxis of memory has consequences for the future of national communities.

The Praxis of Public Memory

The aftermath of a national traumatic event creates the conditions for the psycho-social process of healing and moving on, but it is also the occasion for civic deliberation about what constitutes national identity. The memory of tragic events often becomes the foundation of a nation's new identity.[4] Of these events, Ricoeur (1988) said,

I have in mind those events that a historical community holds to be significant because it sees in them an origin, a return to its beginnings. These events, which are said to be "epoch-making," draw their specific meaning from their capacity to found or reinforce the community's consciousness of identity, its narrative identity, as well as the identity of its members. These events generate feelings of considerable ethical intensity, whether this be fervent commemoration or some manifestation of loathing, or indignation, or of regret or compassion, or even the call for forgiveness. (p. 187)

It is perhaps because of this ethical tension the past brings into the present that memory is both feared and revered. As James Booth (2006) argues, this tension can be the source of conflict and violence but it is also central to national reconciliation and justice. On the one hand, as David Lowenthal (1996) suggests, there is an obsession with memory because people today are obsessed with their past–for better or for worse.[5] On the other hand, Pierre Nora, editor of *The Realms of Memory* (Les Lieux de la Memoire), argues, "we speak so much of memory because there is so little of it left" (qtd. in Gillis, 1994, p. 7). Nora is referring here specifically to memory sustained through orality the vernacular type of memory, not the official or commercialized.

Public memory is constituted at various levels and through different mediums or "realms," as Pierre Nora refers to them. It also needs to be distinguished from both collective and social types of memory. Maurice Halbwachs (1992), whose argument originated from Emile Durkheim's idea of collective conscience, introduced the notion of collective memory in the early twentieth century. He suggests that all acts of memory or remembrance are necessarily social; that is, when one remembers an event, one does it as part of a collectivity. In other words, to speak about public memory is to speak about acts performed in the public realm that rely on remembering. Commemorative activity is "by definition social and political, for it involves the coordination of individual and group memories, whose results may appear consensual when they are in fact the product of processes of intense contest, struggle, and, in some instances, annihilation" (Gillis, 1994, p. 5). Engaging in remembrance is a difficult endeavor for a community precisely because each person remembers and interprets past events differently.

Renewed scholarly interest in memory originated in the debates about significant events in recent history, such as the two

World Wars, the Jewish Holocaust, and the Russian Revolution, to mention a few. This interest is also evident in the significant body of scholarship that focuses on issues of identity, collective/public memory, and nationalism. Jeffrey Barash (1997) points out,

> One of the chief sources of the historian's recent interest in memory has been the historian's conflict (Historikersteit) of the 1980s concerning the interpretation of the German and European past since the rise of the power of Nazism and in the aftermath of World War II. As the generations who lived through and–from a given perspective–remembered these events increasingly pass away, the question concerning the precise historical meaning has reemerged with a new urgency. (p. 708)

This statement illustrates how history functions to make sense of past events, and how memory, that of witnesses in particular, is central to the process. Indeed, Patrick Hutton (1993) argues that history constitutes an art of memory

> because it mediates the encounter between two moments of memory: repetition and recollection. Repetition concerns the presence of the past. It is the moment of memory through which we bear forward images of the past that continue to shape our present efforts to evoke the past. It is the moment of memory with which we consciously reconstruct images of the past in the selective way that suits the need of our present situation. It is the opening between these two moments that makes historical thinking possible. (p. xxi)

Hutton (1993) also discusses the different approaches that have been taken historically in the discussion about the connection between history and memory. Drawing on Kierkegaard's dual conception of memory–memory being both the child's memory and the old man's recollection–Hutton frames the relationship between memory and history within the metaphor of the Nook of Eight Path. These paths include the following aspects of memory: rhetorical, autobiographical, psychological, sociological, archeological, historical, mnemonic, and historiographical. The increase in commemorative practices around the globe is also a case in point.

There are, therefore, various definitions or interpretations of what a historian's work or historical endeavor entails or means. In postmodernity, the task of the historian has shifted from a "simple" process of recreation of the past that constructed a fluid connection between memory and history to a more delicate conception of the task of the historian in which issues of interpretation, dialogue, historicity, and ethics are central (Hutton, 1993). Of postmodern historians, Hutton (1993) notes, "They are more suspicious of the distortions of memory, and they are watchful of the transference of their own memories onto the histories that they would write" (p. 535). Memory is often conceived as the authentic location of what one's past experiences and knowledge, whereas history is more of a linguistic construct that uses memory but also abuses it. This tension between history and memory is captured here by Nora's *The Realms of Memory*. According to Nora (1996),

> Memory is life, always embodied in living societies and as such in permanent evolution, subject to the dialectic of remembering and forgetting, unconscious of the distortions to which it is subject, vulnerable in various ways to appropriation and manipulation, and capable of lying dormant for long periods of time only to be suddenly reawakened. History, on the other hand, is the reconstruction, always problematic and incomplete, of what is no longer. Memory is always a phenomenon of the present, a bond tying us to the eternal present; history is a representation of the past... Memory situates remembrance in a sacred context. History ferrets it out; it turns whatever it touches into prose....Memory is rooted in the concrete: in space, gesture, image and object. History dwells exclusively on temporal continuities, on changes in things and in the relations among things. Memory is absolute, while history is always relative. (p. 3)

Memory is sacred, subjective, yet absolute: memory as life, as history, in contrast, is the attempt, always relative, to finalize everything, to freeze the past into a comprehensive account.

Public memories are numerous and can be found in geographical places, historical monuments, buildings, literary works, art forms, commemorations, symbols, and other genres and practices that suggest an audience. But the metaphor of public memory also implies a dual temporal configuration, as Edward Casey (2004) emphasizes,

> Public memory is both attached to the past (typically an originating event of some sort) and acts to ensure a future of further remembering of that same event. Public monuments embody this Janusian trait: their very massiveness and solidity almost literally enforce this futurity, while inscriptions and certain easily identifiable features (for example, the giant seated Abraham Lincoln of the Lincoln Memorial) pull the same physical object toward the past it honors. (p. 17)

This view of public memory reveals the ambiguous and complex character of any attempt to capture the past. The past is not only elusive, fragmentary, and disputatious, as Matt Matsuda (1996) suggests, but it is also prone to all kinds of appropriations and misappropriations. Public memory is then also political. In *Remaking America: Public Memory, Commemoration, and Patriotism in the Twentieth Century*, John Bodnar (1992) provides an account of the construction of public memory in the United States and suggests interesting connections between public memory, collective identity, and politics. For Bodnar, public memory is above all a rhetorical and political phenomenon; it is a struggle for power between official and vernacular cultures to assign meaning to the past and, ultimately, to shape the present.

Similarly, Booth (2006) sees strong connections between the drive to make sense of the past and a community's identity. Memory seeks to keep the past alive by projecting it in the present: "[I]t [memory] is at once a defensive struggle to preserve a connection with the absent and the dense soil of habit and institutional memory, that almost effortless infusion of the past into the present" (p. xi). The kinship between memory and identity is evident for both individuals and groups. In a family setting, for example, this connection is explained by the need to maintain the tradition and secure the continuity of the family's identity. The identity of larger communities too relies on memory for both continuity and change and, most importantly, to ensure that (some kind of) justice is served. According to Booth (2006),

> Memory-identity matters because, among other things, it is the ground of imputation, of the society (or person) as owner of its past and responsible for it, as well as identical to, and thus capable of, making commitments to a future, of binding its future by a present promise. And because we are members of a persisting and accountable community, we bear witness. That is, we seek to ensure through acts of memory a certain persistence of the crime, the victim, and the perpetrator. (p. xiii)

Testimonies spoken in communities with a past of injustice and suffering, such as Morocco, are in this sense not only realms of memories but also a significant aspect of the public memory of a people. These narratives seek to assign meaning to the past, reshape a people's identity, and serve justice by recognizing an injustice, the perpetrator of the injustice and, most importantly, the victim. But what does it mean to be a victim in this context? Casey (2004) argues,

A victim is a public person–if not yet explicitly so, then potentially so (that is, as someone who can be recognized as such, present a case in court, complain in public, etc.). Precisely because a victim cannot argue for himself–because he is dead or lacks the knowledge or resources to become a plaintiff–public testimonial is the more requisite if that person (however unknown to the public initially, however much stranger) is to reclaim recognition or vindication. Without the testimonial, verbal and/or pictorial, the victim recedes into oblivion, remembered only by his or her family and friends–and thus part of individual and social memory–but not belonging expressly to public memory, at most a cipher or empty number in that memory (that is, as just one among the many dead as currently counted). (p. 20)

Testimonies give a human face to the past, and they ensure that the past does not fall into oblivion, and that it is transmitted to future generations. They can provide, as Priscilla B. Hayner (2002) recommends, the opportunity for a nation to remember to forget. Testimonies provide the opportunity for deliberation not just about past actions (responsibility, accountability, and justice) but also about possibilities for the future of a people (identity, constitution).

Along with public memory, a discussion of Ricoeur's philosophy will frame the issues discussed earlier in light of narrative theory and communication ethics. As a vernacular form of history, public memory is important to consider in light of Ricoeur's argument that the identity of individuals as well as communities is constituted narratively, and that the (historical) present we inhabit is always constituted within a dialectic between a space of experience (ideology, past) and a horizon of expectation (utopia, future). Keeping this dialectic alive is tantamount to a healthy political community. Along with Ricoeur, Richard Kearney (2004) argues that the tension between belonging (past) and distance (future) is helpful as "cut off from one another, they run the risk of pathological extremes: ideology imprisoning us in reactionary conservatism, utopia sacrificing us to a schizophrenic image of an abstract future without the conditions for its realization" (Kearney, 2004, p. 7).

Paul Ricoeur: Narrative Identity and the Past

Ricoeur's work spans over half a century and addresses a wide range of philosophical questions and concerns. Perhaps, he is most recognized for his contribution to the "hermeneutic turn" as well as his continuous "interpretation of the 'mediations' of meaning through symbol, myth, dream, image, text, narrative and ideology" (Kearney, 2004, p. 13). If one were tempted to find an intellectual thread (or hermeneutic entrance) to his thought, the concept of narrative and narrative identity would be a promising path. As Peter Kemp and David Rasmussen (1989) argue, narrative theory is the backbone of Ricoeur's ethical theory. Ricoeur cannot understand or even conceive of ethics outside of a narrative framework. Yet, despite its rhetorical and philosophical value, Ricoeur's work on memory has not yet been fully appreciated. Andreea Deciu Ritivoi (2006), a scholar committed to bringing Ricoeur into the rhetorical tradition, points out that "Ricoeur's endeavors in moral and political philosophy, or more recently in memory studies have received little attention from rhetorical scholars, although they elaborate and clarify his work in hermeneutics and in the philosophy of language" (p. 3).

The work that is perhaps most familiar to rhetoricians is the three volumes of *Time and Narrative* (1984, 1985, 1988), in which Ricoeur posited a narrative framework as a potential antidote to the aporia of time. Granting the relevance of this work, we should also consider the importance of *Oneself as Another* (1992), in which Ricoeur fully explicated the connection between narrative and ethics, and expanded his narrative theory to personal identity. Further, Memory, History, Forgetting (2004) engages a lacuna left in *Time and Narrative,* and *Oneself as Another,* as Ricoeur (2004) noted by stating, in effect, that when one speaks of temporal experience and narrative, it is important not to overlook memory and forgetting, which constitute, he argues, "the median levels between time and narrative" (p. xv).

Narrative theory is helpful in understanding the linkages between time, identity, and selfhood and their ethical implications. Ricoeur (1984) began his treatise on time and narrative by stating,

> The world unfolded by every narrative work is always a temporal world. Or, as will often be repeated in the course of this study: time becomes human time to the extent that it is organized after the manner of a narrative; narrative, in turn, is meaningful to the extent that it portrays the features of temporal experience. (p. 1)

This statement suggests a symbiotic relationship between temporal categories and narrative. Narration is the (temporary) answer to the aporia of time, mediating between Augustine's cosmological time and Husserl's phenomenology of time: "Narrated time is like a bridge set over the breach speculation constantly opens between phenomenological time and cosmological time" (Ricoeur, 1988, p. 244).

Both conceptions of time are helpful and need not be mutually exclusive, since human beings experience time as both cosmological time and phenomenological time. Bridging the gap between these different approaches becomes a task that Ricoeur takes up in *Time and Narrative* because time provides a window into the meaning of human existence. It is, of course, in stories that time ceases to be an abstract idea and becomes human. The past, for instance, is no longer a "foreign country" when it is recounted in historical texts where one can imagine it or, in some sense, get close to it. Indeed, narration (or a poetics of narrative) does indirectly mediate between these two experiences of time by positing a "third-time," a category that is derived from ontology of history: historical time. History is not the only narrative form that "humanizes" time alone; fictional narrative does too, and thus both history and fiction, Ricoeur (1988) argues, must be considered as a dialectic because of "the criss-crossing processes of a fictionalization of history and a historization of fiction" (p. 246). It is the marriage of these two creative temporal structures that gives birth to the metaphor of "narrative identity," an identity that can be assigned to a person or a people (Ricoeur, 1988, p. 246).

Narrative identity is an attempt to overcome the philosophical impasse caused by thinking about personal identity:

> Without recourse to narration, the problem of personal identity would in fact be condemned to an antimony with no solution. Either we must posit a subject identical with itself through the diversity of its different states, or, following Hume or Nietzsche, we must hold that this identical subject is nothing more than a substantialist illusion, whose elimination merely brings to light a pure manifold of cognitions, emotions, and volitions. This dilemma disappears if we substitute for identity understood in the sense of being the same (idem), identity understood in the sense of oneself as self-same [soi-meme] (ipse). (Ricoeur, 1988, p. 246)

This initial understanding of narrative identity (as discussed in *Time and Narrative*) is threefold: First, the self understands itself via interpretation; second, this interpretation is mediated primarily through narrative, among other signs and symbols; and third, narration combines history and fiction for the construction of a life story (Ricoeur, 1992, p. 114 n.1). It is, in many ways, the result of a circular relationship between a person or a community's historical experience and the narration that results from such experience.

This hermeneutic circle is not a closed circle since identity is never stagnant or dead; it is always shifting and changing.

Personal identity can be conceived in terms of sameness and self-hood, and also in terms of narrative identity's mediation between action theory and moral theory. On the notion of emplotment developed by Aristotle, Ricoeur explained the movement of narrative identity between identity (sameness) and diversity. This dialectic between sameness and diversity becomes the ethical component of Ricoeur's theory of narrative identity. For Ricoeur (1992), "there is no ethically neutral narrative" (p. 115). The ethical implications of narrative identity stem from the interconnectedness of identity and action: our actions describe who we are.

Narration refers necessarily to human action. When, for example, a witness in Morocco tells about her experience of political violence, she is referring to actions, by her and by others. Her story both describes the past and evaluates it. Human action can, in fact, be approached in three modes of language, what Ricoeur (1992) calls the polysemy of action: description, narration, and prescription. Narration is both descriptive and prescriptive. What is then so important about narration is that it brings together action and language, two important coordinates in Ricoeur's philosophy. John Hatch (2006) rightly points out that "Ricoeur does not view language primarily as an instrument of human agency that separates us from our 'natural' condition and imposes order(s), but as the medium in which we creatively (re)construct our lives as stories 'with and for others'" (p. 5). Stories, whether fictional or historical, open up readers to a world of possibilities, but each possibility is pregnant with ethical implications.

Such is the past of nations and peoples; actions, waiting to be read and interpreted. The interpretation and representation of a nation's past, with all the struggles and conflicts such a process brings about, may constitute a community's ethical awakening. For a people to engage in interpretation of the past is to respond to a promise made to their predecessors; it is part of a process of self-understanding. To dismiss the past or forget it is to be, in a way, a historical orphan, a people without a beginning or a trace; in brief, it constitutes historical homelessness. The implications for a community's identity, as Ricoeur understands it, are significant: "[n]arrative identity...is not just a psychological construct, but a composite of detailed memory and present re-evaluation. Narrative is both testament to the diversity of past human accomplishment and the possible basis for further self-determination" (Joy, 1997, p. xxii).

The dialectic of the past and the future is most manifest in the importance that we give to history or historical work. Historians are entrusted with the mission of telling us about the past, in all truth, so that we learn how people before us lived. History for Ricoeur (2004) is the rediscovery of the "dialectic of the past and the future and exchanges in the present" (p. 343). He also suggests that the "making" of history is taking place in the present for the present (a present pregnant with the past) and certainly for the future. Ricoeur warns, however, that the present is not to be reduced to presence. The present should be the time of initiative and responsible decisions when "ordinary" people allow their memories to speak so that the unspeakable becomes public and does not fall into oblivion. Witnesses, like those who recently took part in the public testimonies in Morocco after the new political leadership opened public discussions,[6] narrated their own stories, and the stories of friends or family members, in an act of courage, as an ethical call, political obligation, and often both.

History is a narrative about the suffering of our predecessors, as both Ricoeur and Hannah Arendt suggested. In fact, one of Arendt's (1973) critiques of modern history is that it lost touch with its original raison d'etre, in that it no longer concerned itself with the sufferings of human beings. Human suffering, Ricoeur (1988) suggested, is a necessary result of action: "it is within the dimension of acting (and suffering which is a corollary) that thought about history will bring together its perspectives within the horizon of the idea of an imperfect mediation" (p. 208). It is perhaps necessary to point out that suffering is not always a physical experience or, perhaps, not solely a physical or even psychological pain. Suffering occurs when one's capacity for action is diminished, violated, or destroyed. In other words, to suffer is to be incapacitated, to be denied the capacity to act, and be responsible for one's actions (Ricoeur, 1992). One's share of power is eviscerated in instances of suffering, and one's ability to make public that which has forestalled the capacity to act is challenged when the superiority of the other's authority is not mollified by a recognition of fragility, or even mortality.

Still, for Ricoeur (2004), the line between victim and agent can be blurred, as one is inevitably both an agent and a victim of history:

We are only the agents of history inasmuch as we also suffer it. The victims of history and the innumerable masses who, still today, undergo history more than they make it are the witnesses par excellence to this major structure of our historical condition. And those who are–or who believe themselves to be–the most active agents of history suffer it no less than do its–or their–victims, even if this only be in terms of the unintended effects of their most calculated enterprises. (p. 216)

This conception of history is linked to a sense of justice, a crucial concept in Ricoeur's ethical theory. It is often a sense of justice, or more accurately, a sense of injustice, that compels one to tell a story of a relative or a friend, have his or her side of the story heard and made public. Justice is not reducible to interpersonal relations, but it is through these relations that the just and unjust play out their stakes. And what maintains the just or the unjust is largely determined by individuals who are able to judge particular instances, a judgment that sometimes hinges on a sensibility that supersedes the normative. This extralegal or extranormative sense of justice expresses a practical wisdom that is cultivated both individually and communally, and that emphasizes "the need to move from moral norms per se to the ethical aim of norms" (Muldoon, 2002, p. 95).

For Ricoeur, the normative (morality) is not to be confused with the ethical. A distinction between ethics and morality presupposes the temporal and narrative constraints presented in *Time and Narrative*. In *Oneself as Another*, Ricoeur (1992) advanced a distinctive notion of an ethical life grounded in the relations between obligation to others and the pursuit of the good life. In advancing the teleological aim of the accomplished life and the deontological claim for obligation to respect the moral norm, he argued for three theses:

(1) the primacy of ethics over morality, (2) the necessity of ethics to pass through the sieve of the norm, and (3) the legitimacy of recourse by the norm to the aim whenever the norm leads to impasses in practice-impasses recalling at this new stage of our meditation the various aporetic situations which our reflection on selfhood has had to face. Ethics are more fundamental than any norm. (p. 170)

The ethical practice necessary for the actualization of the good life cannot be conceived outside of historical, political, social, and individual contexts and requires practical wisdom. Ricoeur (1992) stated that "[p]ractical wisdom consists in inventing conduct that will best satisfy the exception required by solicitude...What practical wisdom most requires in...ambiguous cases is a meditation on the relation between happiness and suffering" (p. 269). The present offers the opportunity for mediation between happiness and suffering, between past and future. The present should become the time of initiative and responsible decisions not only about the past but also for the future. It is at this junction that memory, understood as the thread that links a person or a community to the past, becomes significant. Public memory, as witnessed through public displays of testimony in Morocco, offers a praxial perspective that demonstrates my argument that public memory is necessary to link people and communities together.

Testimonies as Public Memory: Speaking about the "Years of Lead" in Morocco

Morocco is a country with multiple identities–Arab, Amazigh, Jewish, Muslim, and African–who have cohabitated for many centuries, at times in conflict, but at relative peace for much of the past 100 years. The political system is referred to as a constitutional monarchy, with a king (Mohammed VI) who belongs to a dynasty that has ruled Morocco since the seventeenth century. As Susan Slyomovics (2005) points out in *The Performance of Human Rights in Morocco*, the only time that the rule of the Alaouite dynasty (to which the current king belongs) was seriously undermined was during French colonial rule, between 1912 and 1956. Since Morocco gained independence in 1956, the country has experienced great political turmoil. In the course of the past 50 years, the Moroccan State has arrested, tortured, kidnapped, exiled, and executed thousands of its citizens. The violence has targeted people across all ethnic (Arab, Amazigh, and Jewish), religious (Muslim, Jewish, and nonreligious), and gender lines as well as political affiliations. Any person or group that presented a political opinion that ran against the official line was deemed a threat and dealt with violently. In other words, the policy of the State from the 1960s through the 1980s, commonly referred to by Moroccans as the "years of lead" (in reference to the lead in bullets), was one of a zero tolerance for dissent.[7]

In the early 1990s, owing to international pressure and in an effort for damage control to the public image of Morocco, the monarch (Hassan II) who ascended to the throne in 1961 determined that it was time to introduce changes. These changes included an acknowledgment of the existence of secret prisons (Tazmamart in particular), the release of selected political prisoners, and a loosening of constraints on public discourse. The other notable change in the management of political affairs was the introduction of the concept of human rights into the rhetoric of the State. This act was accompanied, first, by the establishment of an official organization for the assessment of the human rights situation in the country, and later the creation of a Ministry of Human Rights, which no longer exists, as it was deemed that the human rights situation in Morocco no longer needed redress. The introduction of the discourse of human rights into the State's rhetoric did not match the political practice in the streets, however, as arbitrary arrests and disappearances continued.[8] As Abdeslam Maghraoui (2003) points out, "Morocco is no closer today to a decisive democratic breakthrough than it was four decades ago" (p. 73).

In 1999, with the death of King Hassan II and the enthroning of his son, Mohammed VI, the new monarch put the redemption of postcolonial Moroccan history on a fast track. He ordered the creation of an indemnification commission to compensate those people (or the families in case the victim was deceased) who were deemed, through their account, to be victims of wrongs perpetrated by officials acting in the name of the State. This type of initiative was not a historical novelty; according to Slyomovics (2005), "[t]he creation of a Moroccan Indemnity Commission owes much to the unprecedented legal history of the Nuremberg war crimes trials and German redress programs to victims of Nazi persecution in the aftermath of World War II" (p. 26). This commission was not the first of its kind in Morocco but it was the first royal initiative to address wrongs of the past committed by the State.[9] The most important new development was the creation of the Commission for Equity and Reconciliation (IER), established by royal decree in late 2003. It ended its mandate earlier in 2006.

Like every singular experience, the Moroccan experience of reckoning with its past is unique, but there are, of course, similarities with other experiences that should not be overlooked. Andrew Wolpert (2001) points out, "comparison is useful also because...[it] can help us better appreciate and contextualize how others come to terms with the disturbing and unsettling events of their past" (p. xviii). For instance, similar to South Africa, it appears that the Moroccan State is using the rhetoric of reconciliation as a catalyst for national unity and political change. The mandate of the IER has been to (1) establish the truth through testimonies and interviews with victims and their families, (2) provide recommendations aimed to preserve public memory and guarantee a genuine rupture with the abusive practices of the past, erase the scars of the violations, and restore and reinforce trust in the State and respect of human rights, and (3) foster reconciliation, defined as "the contribution to the culture of dialogue in order to consolidate the democratic transition and a state where the law rules, in order to promote civic values and a culture of human rights."[10] The State's proposed project of reconciliation is thus intimately linked with its rhetoric of democratic transition. However, far from meeting with unanimity, the Moroccan project has ignited controversy about the meaning of several practices (or what these practices entail) and conceptions, such as reconciliation, memorialization, equity, and forgiveness.[11]

Despite the controversy and conflicts that emerged in the wake of these developments, there are at least two positive aspects. First, for many victims and their families, the purpose for this laborious undertaking is to uncover the truth so that their stories are recorded as part of the country's history. Widad Bouab, a former female political prisoner who testified in the official hearings, states,

> I believe that true reconciliation can only happen through access to truth... That is why I accepted to testify, to inform public opinion of what was going on during the years of lead and what we endured because of our opinions. The purpose of my testimony was to make this information, this history, public and to denounce it...these are traces that could contribute to the unveiling of truth, traces for my people. (Personal communication, July 2006)

For Bouab and many other Moroccans, to narrate one's experience of violence is to inscribe it in public memory and history. Indeed, Ricoeur (2004) argued that testimonies are part of the process of making history: "With testimony opens an epistemological process that departs from declared memory, passes through the archive and documents, and finds its fulfillment in documentary proof" (p. 161). In other words, to know and record one's history is important for epistemological reasons, at the least. Moroccan citizens who are part of this discussion are thus trying to understand, judge, and learn from their past so that such past is neither revisited nor comes back to haunt them, as is the case in Spain (the pact of oblivion) and with undigested issues of slavery in the United States.

The past has been a "foreign land" for most citizens for a long time, because either they were never informed of what was taking place in their country in terms of treatment of their fellow citizens or, if they were informed, they were paralyzed with fear. In other words, before the creation of this commission, to speak of the past meant to be political and to be political meant, in effect, that one could be subject to State violence. Maghraoui (2003) argues that through a policy of violence and strategic political moves, the Moroccan monarchy had managed to depoliticize its citizenry. If this argument is valid, then the potential for this display of memory is immense as it may contribute to a reengaging of citizens. For political transition (to democracy) to take place, citizens need to be fully engaged in politics and assert their presence in the public sphere. Speaking about the work of the IER, its president, Driss Benzekri, states, "It is not only a matter of sharing knowledge and appropriation of the past but also to create in the present (through debate) norms and rules for living together and build a future."[12] This narrative is a representation or mimesis of the past actions of a people (ethnos); it defines their ethos and identity, past, present, and future; it articulates their "presence in the world" (Kearney, 2004, p. 158).

Kay Schaffer and Sidonie Smith (2006) argue that acts of telling (a story) about one's experience of state-sponsored violence have been efficacious in compelling a moral response from local and international audiences. They state,

> These acts of remembering test the values that nations profess to live by against the actual experiences and perceptions of the storyteller as witness. They issue an ethical call to listeners both within and beyond national borders to recognize the disjunction between the values espoused by the community and the actual practices that occur. They issue a call...to respond to the story; to recognize the humanity of the teller and the justice of the claim; to take responsibility for that recognition; and to find means of redress. (p. 3)

Through their testimony, victims of violence appeal to their audience's sense of justice through pathos and ethos. Such an appeal demands not only a listener but also a response. In Morocco, there has been an outpouring of testimonies and victims' narratives about the "years of lead."

Several of these stories were presented through official channels, namely in public testimonies organized by the IER. Slyomovics (2005) argues that with Moroccan narratives of suffering, like with other such narratives, "the value and worth of a man or a woman can be provisionally quantified" (p. 28). Because of the link established between testifying (telling one's story of victimhood) and obtaining reparations (for one's suffering or a family member's death), human life and worth can thus be put in dollar terms. But perhaps such an argument, with its focus on money as a symbol of recognition of a person's unjust treatment, distracts from the more significant contribution of witnesses and their testimonies.

Similarly, models that focus primarily on the cathartic and traumatic aspects of testimonies often do not fully take into account the ethico-political and pragmatic implications of these events. Schaffer and Smith (2006) argue that the psychoanalytical model has been the dominant framework in the West for thinking about and explaining stories that speak of political violence. Although the psychological aspects of experiences of abuse and trauma are certainly important, they remain personal. When a citizen presents his or her experience of being a victim of State violence in a public forum, his/her narrative moves from the private to the public realm; to testify is an ethico-political act with implications for the individual citizen as well as the national community. It is about how the narrative of the past as told by one or more citizens contributes to the ongoing reshaping of a people's national identity. Hence, it is important to consider such acts of remembrance in their larger public context.

Conclusion

Ronald C. Arnett states (2007), "The hero walks within stories. The hero extends stories. Only the willingness to walk from private to public accountability makes the hero possible" (p. 82). Though perhaps not part of official history, vernacular narratives about the past do shape the future of a national community—thanks to heroes such as those Arnett defines. It is the act of moving from the personal and private struggle with demons of the past to the public telling and sharing of that past that permits different histories to emerge. Without such acts of courage, the story would be incomplete. But not all those who suffer atrocities at the hands of a tyrannical or genocidal State are provided with the opportunity to testify on what they bore witness to, as many have died, disappeared, been exiled, or otherwise resist confronting the aftermath of their ordeal. People who insist on telling their story are moral witnesses whose contribution is significant not only for the rest of us who did not know or for the traces they offer the historian but for them as well as victims, as citizens who need a voice, an outlet for their suffering and that of those who did not survive.

To be a moral witness is to regain a sense of power-in-common as a citizen of a particular nation and dignity as a human being. Avishai Margalit (2004) states, "The paradigmatic case of a moral witness is one who experiences the suffering–one who is not just an observer, but also a sufferer" (p. 150). A moral witness is the paradigmatic case of how the ethics of narration and the praxis of public memory coincide, and this public memory is the link that provides the ground on which narratives flourish. Public memory permits a conversation about the meaning of the past and an exercise in judgment/judging either as an actor ("judging in order to act") or a spectator ("judging on order to cull meaning from the past") (Benhabib, 1992, p. 121). In other words, testimonies such as those presented in Morocco invite a dialogical consciousness of memory that demands ethical action. Recalling the works of Paul Ricoeur and Gerard Hauser remind us that memory is important but that public memory is essential to continuing ethical human engagement.

Notes

1   The Years of Lead in Morocco refer to the rule of King Hassan II, from the mid-1960s to mid-1990s. The metaphor of lead refers to bullets.

2   Ricoeur points out that "the definition of narrative as 'mimesis of action' or 'acting persons' would emerge reinforced by the addition of suffering to action, whether it be a matter of redefining mimesis as 're-creation', catharsis as 'release', phronesis as 'wisdom', and finally ethos as an 'ethics' concerned with a persisting 'self-identity', which perdures through a life of our memories, projects and presence in the world" (in Kearney, 2004, p. 158).

3   With respect to the different understandings of memory, Blair notes, "This collectivized understanding of memory goes by a number of monikers, including public memory, cultural memory, and social memory. These different names should not be ignored; they signal some significant differenes of intellectual assumption and emphasis. However, what the perspectives represented by these different names have in common is their focus on memory as a collective or communal phenomenon, rather than as an individual, cognitive function" (2006, p. 52).

4   See Paul Ricoeur, Edward Casey, and James Booth.

5　In his book *Possessed by the Past*, David Lowenthal (1996) offers explanations to this modern obsession with the past. Lowenthal argues that, on the one hand, keeping in touch with one's heritage is important but, on the other hand, the obsession with the past can be dangerous, when the past becomes an excuse for all kinds of excesses.

6　These public testimonies will be discussed in more detail later in this chapter.

7　For a detailed account of this and other political developments in Morocco see Andrew R. Smith and Fadoua Loudiy (2005), "Testing the red lines: On the liberalization of speech in Morocco," and Abdeslam Maghraoui, "Depoliticization in Morocco."

8　The Moroccan Association for Human Rights (AMDH) has documented hundreds of human rights abuse cases; the target this time is the Islamists. For details: http://www.amdh.org.ma/ .

9　The first organization to tackle these issues is the nongovernmental organization. See the Forum for Justice and Truth (FJT), [website, www.fvjmaroc.org/fr/] established by a group of former political prisoners, in 1999.

10　See www.ier.ma for my translation.

11　The International Center for Transitional Justice states, "Despite many notable accomplishments, the work of the Commission has not been without its critics who have pointed to its limited investigative powers and the lack of an accountability mechanism for perpetrators of human rights violations. Groups like the Moroccan Association for Human Rights have organized their own versions of public hearings-though without the benefit of national television coverage-in which victims were allowed to name perpetrators. Perhaps the most significant complaints involved the limited information made publicly available by the commission regarding its investigations into the fate of the missing and the burial sites of the deceased. See http://www.ictj.org/en/where/region5/591.html#resources

12　See www.ier.ma

References

Arendt, H. (1973). *Between past and future: Eight exercises in political thought.* New York: Viking Press.

Arnett, R. C. (2007). Hannah Arendt: Dialectical communicative labor. In P. Arneson (Ed.), *Perspectives on philosophy of communication* (pp. 65-88). West Lafayette, IN: Purdue University Press.

Barash, J. (1997). The sources of memory. *Journal of the History of Ideas,* 58 (4), 707-717.

Benhabib, S. (1992). *Situating the self: Gender, community and postmodernism in contemporary ethics.* London: Routledge.

Blair, C. (2006). Collective memory. In G.S. Sheperds, J.S. John & T. Striphas (Eds.), *Communication as....perspectives on theory* (pp. 51-59). Thousand Oaks, CA: Sage.

Bodnar, J. E. (1992). *Remaking America: Public memory, commemoration, and patriotism in the twentieth century.* Princeton, NJ: Princeton University Press.

Booth, W. J. (2006). *Communities of memory: On witness, identity, and justice.*
Ithaca, NY: Cornell University Press.

Casey, E. S. (2004). Public memory in place and time. In K. R. Phillips (Ed.), *Framing public memory* (pp. 17-44). Tuscaloosa: University of Alabama Press.

Gillis, J. (1994). *Commemorations: The politics of national identity.* Princeton, NJ:
Princeton University Press.

Halbwachs, M. (1992). *On collective memory.* (L. A. Coser, Trans.). Chicago: University of Chicago Press.

Hatch, J. (2006). *Between religious visions and secular realities: (Dia)logology and the rhetoric of reconciliation.* Retrieved October 12, 2007, from University of Wisconsin, Madison, Working Papers Library Web site: http://global.wisc.edu/reconciliation/library/papers_open/hatch.html

Hauser, G. (1999). *Vernacular voices: The rhetoric of publics and public spheres.*
Columbia: University of South Carolina Press.

Hayner, P. B. (2002). *Unspeakable truths: Facing the challenge of truth commissions.* New York & London: Routledge.

Hutton, P. (1993). *History as an art of memory.* Burlington: University of Vermont Press.

Hyde, M. J. (2001). *The call of conscience.* Columbia: University of South Carolina Press.

Joy, M. (1997). *Paul Ricoeur and narrative: Context and contestation.* Canada:
University of Calgary Press.

Kearney, R. (2004). *On Paul Ricoeur: The owl of Minerva.* Aldershot, England:
Ashgate Publishing.

Kemp, P., & Rasmussen, D. (Eds.). (1989). *The narrative path: The later works of Paul Ricoeur.* Cambridge, MA: MIT Press.

Lowenthal, D. (1996). *Possessed by the past: The heritage crusade and the spoils of history.* New York: Free Press.

Maghraoui, A. M. (2003). Depoliticization in Morocco. In L. Diamond, M. Plattner,
& D. Brumberg (Eds.), *Islam and democracy in the Middle East* (pp. 67-75).
Baltimore: Johns Hopkins University Press.

Margalit, A. (2004). *The ethics of memory.* Cambridge, MA: Harvard University Press.

Matsuda, M. K. (1996). *The memory of the modern.* Oxford: Oxford University Press.

Muldoon, M. (2002). *On Ricoeur.* London: Wadsworth/Thomson Learning.

Nora, P. (1996). *The realms of memory, vol. 1: Conflicts and divisions.* In P. Nora
(Ed.), New York: Columbia Pres.

Ricoeur, P. (1984). *Time and narrative.* (Vol. 1, K. McLaughin & D. Pellauer,
Trans.). Chicago: University of Chicago Press.

———. (1985). *Time and narrative.* (Vol. 2, K. McLaughin & D. Pellauer, Trans.).
Chicago: University of Chicago Press.

———. (1988). *Time and narrative.* (Vol. 3, K. Blamey & D. Pellauer, Trans.). Chicago: University of Chicago Press.

———. (1992). *Oneself as another.* (K. Blamey, Trans.). Chicago: University of Chicago Press.

———. (2004). *Memory, history, forgetting.* (K. Blamey & D. Pellauer, Trans.). Chicago: University of Chicago Press.

Ritivoi, A. D. (2006). *Paul Ricoeur: Tradition and innovation in rhetorical theory.* Albany: State University of New York Press.

Schaffer, K., & Smith, S. (2006). *Human rights and narrated lives: The ethics of recognition.* New York: Palgrave Macmillan.

Slyomovics, S. (2005). *The performance of human rights in Morocco.* Philadelphia: University of Pennsylvania Press.

Smith, A. R., & Loudiy, F. (2005). Testing the red lines: On the liberalization of speech in Morocco. *Human Rights Quarterly, 27* (3), 1069-1119.

Wolpert, A. (2001). *Remembering defeat: Civil war and civic memory in ancient Athens.* Baltimore: Johns Hopkins University Press.

Chapter 5

Dialogic Meeting: A Constructive Rhetorical Approach to Contemporary Public Relations Practice

John H. Prellwitz

Amid the international tensions, strained relations, and declining trust expressed in various businesses and organizations after a series of corporate scandals and fiscal failures, public relations practice occupies a potentially rich and helpful position in the twenty-first century. As "information work" continues to explode across various new mediums developed by technology, information workers hold the potential to generate and guide communicative action in a constructive manner.

A *dialogic meeting* orientation to public relations offers one such conception of how a reorientation to public relations practice could foster and nurture relationships between publics. Relationships built on trust and strengthened through dialogic encounters that can encourage various publics and organizations to meet problems constructively and creatively are responsive to the opportunities presented by our current moment of fragmented publics. As Leon H. Mayhew (1997) reminds us, "Fragmentation has two faces. What from one perspective is a loss of stable traditional identities is, from another perspective, a gain of freedom to construct new identities and hence new solidarities" (p. 286). Possibilities lie before us to enhance current public relations practice constructively and creatively through a theoretical framework. This framework will be grounded in the demands placed on us as professionals by the current historical moment, and informed by resilient rhetorical and philosophical ideas that call forward these possibilities.

The constructive orientation to public relations practice offered here is grounded in three textured and interrelated areas–history, rhetoric, and the philosophically and discursively rich metaphor of dialogue as conceived by Russian philosopher Mikhail Bakhtin. A constructive approach assumes that we can work to "co-constitu-tively discover the minimal communication background assump-tions necessary to permit persons of difference to shape together the communicative terrain of the twenty-first century" (Arnett & Arneson, 1999, p. 277). Coconstruction implies a need to understand the notion of historicity.

Historicity within our context here refers to "the actors' aware-ness of history and society as human constructions" (Hauser, 1999, p. 116). This does not imply that all meanings are seen as individual creations but also recognizes how culture "provides vocabularies for argument, terms that furnish attached justifications, implied rea-sons, assumed imperatives, and implicit narratives to rhetorical pleas just by framing them in language" (Mayhew, 1997, pp. 45-46). Culture and sociohistorical influences can never be ignored. If culture is not considered when shaping arguments to support and establish communication and subsequent relationships, then a mo-nologic approach ensues.

A monologic approach limits opportunities by denying the exis-tence of the other parties. Bakhtin's (1984) definition of monologism is "words that expect no answer" (p. 63). "Bakhtin emphasizes the fact that every speaker must also be a listener and a respondent" (Vice, 1997, p. 52). With a monologic approach (in its extreme or pure form), another person remains wholly and merely an object of consciousness and not another consciousness. No response is ex-pected from it that could change everything in the world of my con-sciousness. Monologue is finalized and deaf to the other's response. It does not expect it and does not acknowledge in it any decisive force. Monologue manages without the other, and therefore to some degree materializes all reality. "Monologue pretends to be the ulti-mate word. It closes down the represented world and represented persons" (Bakhtin, 1984, p. 293). There is then potential for alienat-ing potential public(s) by ignoring their humanness and address-ing them in a closed manner wherein they serve as means to the ends of another. The culture that frames the arguments appears "to be made for people rather than produced and reproduced by them through their communicative action in pursuit of shared meaning" (Mayhew, 1997, p. 85). Although it is important to respect the agen-cy of all actors, it is also important to recall that one is working in a contingent world where unforeseen meanings can be attached to messages by actions beyond control of any one actor, organization, or public. Such recognition of the swaying and unknown future, which we face in acting in the present, must always guide the adaptive and responsive approach articulated here.

One especially important area to be cognizant of is the dynamic and diverse publics and organizations with which public relations professionals interact. Mayhew (1997) suggests that to coordinate multiple and shifting audiences a speaker must seek to establish trust between parties, whereby audiences credit to the speaker the assumption that he or she speaks honestly. If demanded, the speaker will disclose the evidence and warrants for his/her claims. Leonara Black and Charmaine E. J. Härtel (2002) reinforce this notion, asserting that effective and ethical communication "requires openness and a willingness to disclose information that is crucial to the relationship" (p. 12). This process subsequently works not from a model of an assumed public but rather "with a process-oriented concept of a public engaged in learning" (Mayhew, 1997, p. 254) as discussed further in the following text.

Bakhtin and Dialogic Meeting

To engage such malleable and dynamic publics through information work, the metaphor of dialogic meeting is offered to foster and nurture relationships between publics and organizations through ethical communicative behaviors. The theory that informs the communicative actions advocated here is culled from the writings of Russian philosopher Mikhail Bakhtin. For Bakhtin (1984), "[t]o be means to communicate" (p. 287). Meaning emerges in dialogue through the change of a speaking subject. It is through this dynamic interplay of voices that meaning arises, through the process of dialogue (Bakhtin, 1986, pp. 92-93). Therefore, Michael Holquist (1990) notes that the being of each speaking subject engaged in dialogue is then one of "co-being," "an event that is shared. Being is a simultaneity; it is always co-being" (p. 25). The shared nature of co-being influences meaning construction through meeting that occurs in the space opened for communication by a dialogic orientation.

However, Holquist (1990) states that this is not to mean that dialogue is a dyadic structure, rather it is triadic. A dialogue is

> composed of an utterance, a reply, and a relation between the two. It is the relation that is the most important of the three, for without it the other two would have no meaning. They would be isolated, and the most primary of Bakhtinian a prioris is that nothing is anything in itself. (p. 38)

This recognition of shared existence signals the importance of developing relationships through dialogic meeting. Dialogic meeting seeks to encourage relationships between parties through honest and open communication and action. Accordingly, "at the heart of any dialogue is the conviction that what is exchanged has meaning" and that each speaker assumes that somewhere out there exists a future possible addressee "who will understand" (Holquist, 1990, p. 38). Exchange of meaning and establishment of understanding will help to reinforce the ground of potential relationships between organizations and publics.

Meeting brings a dialogic orientation to the activity of discourse, its preparation, delivery, and subsequent interpretation and reinterpretation by organizations, information workers, and diverse publics and audiences. Recognizing dialogue as a process of encounter facilitates a deeper union of word and deed-enhancing the coconstruction of meaning and affording greater opportunity for ethical persuasion. In this manner, activity reveals discourse through meeting. Transparency grows through meeting in the shared communicative activity of discourse as the coconstruction of meaning.

Bakhtin (1991) further explains the glaring importance of recognizing meaning as becoming within the sociohistorical context through his concept of heteroglossia. Heteroglossia, as presented in *The Dialogic Imagination*, is the

> base condition governing the utterance. It is that which insures the primacy of context over text. At any given time, in any given place, there will be a set of conditions, social, historical, meteorological, physiological that will insure that a word uttered in that place and at that time will have a meaning different than it would have under any other conditions. (Bakhtin, 1991, p. 438)

It is this layering of meaning through communication and this necessary recognition of the dialogues behind a specific dialogue, "that permit language to be used in ways that are indirect, conditional, distanced" (Bakhtin, 1991, p. 323). Heteroglossia is therefore properly described as a quality of language itself that is necessarily various. "The authentic environment of an utterance, the environment in which it lives and takes shape, is dialogized heteroglossia, anonymous and social as language, but simultaneously concrete, filled with specific content and accented as an individual utterance" (Bakhtin, 1991, p. 272). "The word in language is half someone else's" (Bakhtin, 1991, p. 293). The dual nature of discourse power-fully informs how social forces always affect the messages public relations professionals craft. The successful campaign depends not only on the knowledge and art of the information work but also on the active understanding and response of the audience.

Bakhtin's dialogic orientation situates the person or public, in our context, not as a means but as an end. The communication that emerges through a dialogic orientation builds on the relationship shared to constitute and communicate meaning. This parallels how praxis, theory-informed action, is combined here to offer a theory-informed idea of a dialogic meeting orientation to public relations that integrates theory and action.

Theory can be incarnated only in responsible action. Actions engaged within a centripetal vacuum, without recourse to the other cannot be seen as embodied, as being, greatly reducing the possibility for the emergence of constructive relationships. It is against this potentially destructive and oppressive monologic rhetoric that Bakhtin (1991) opposes heteroglossia, the centrifugal force, the "counterbalance to centralizing language" (p. 85). Owing to its situatedness within the sociocultural moment, it is, while the centripetal monologue remains nonbeing, an abstract, spectral ideology of the mind.

Dialogic meeting does not deny the persuasive appeals of public relations work. It enjoins the various interests of groups to promote the establishment and enhancement of understanding through reliance on rhetorical argument to influence parties to the advantages of coparticipation in mutually enriching communication and relationships. As Hauser (1999) notes, the primary purpose becomes the "constitution of discursive spaces with the capacity to encourage and nurture a multilogue across their respective borders and from which civil judgments sustainable in multiple perspectives may emerge" (p. 74). The possibility of enjoining organizations and publics rests within one's rhetorical knowledge and ability to understand and apply ideas and information to promote these ends.

Meeting Rhetoric in Dialogue

Rhetoric, in the context of this discussion, refers "not only to suasive discourse but also to a method for thinking about communication, especially its heuristic concerns for invention" (Hauser, 1999, p. 33). This builds upon the responsive nature of dialogue put forth by Bakhtin. As Gerard A. Hauser (1999) notes, "Invention's animus includes taking the audience's vantage point into account" (p. 33). This highlights the rhetorical character of publics themselves as well:

> [A]ny given public exists in its publicness, which is to say in its rhetorical
> character.... In short, the ability to participate in rhetorical exchanges, to
> have rhetorical experiences, requires a certain sort of subjectivity. It is a
> subjectivity unlike that found in interest groups, whose members often
> proceed on closed-minded assumptions of the wholly knowing. Whether
> attention to social exchange alters or reinforces personal views, collective
> participation in rhetorical processes *constitutes individuals as a public.*
> (1999, pp. 32-34)

Hauser's comments illustrate the close relationship between dialogue and rhetoric. Invention illuminates the social and rhetorical character of publics whose constitution is defined by openness to communication rather than monologic demagoguery in which people are manipulated to achieve closed ends rather than to foster textured communication and enduring relationships of consequence.

The ability to perceive how to craft effective and ethical appeals alludes to the rich Aristotelian tradition from which this rhetorical perspective originates. Such an approach builds on Aristotle's (1991) seminal definition of rhetoric as the "ability, in each [particular] case, to see the available means of persuasion" (pp. 36-37). This presupposes that observation is not an immediate, a priori action. In other words, it is not the technique-driven approach of a mechanic who changes part after part on a car until he or she gets it right. Rather, a responsive dialogic orientation exists wherein one first listens, then seeks to enter and influence the current of the conversation in which he or she has engaged.

Given this prescriptive preamble, what is the significance of an orientation to public relations practice? Within the horizons of this discussion, the philosophical and theoretical foundation for public relations practice will be at the foreground. The day-to-day communicative actions engaged to meet deadlines and demands will not be engaged. However, we address contributions that the philosophical and rhetorical orientation to public relations presented here may cast on pragmatic and strategic elements of public relations as communicative behavior enacted through both word and deed.

Carol H. Botan and Francisco Soto (1995) position public relations under the aegis of strategic communication (p. 23). This allows for a broad understanding of how public relations functions "as a paradigmatic example of strategic communication" (Botan & Soto, 1995, p. 23) including a wide array of purposes, ranging from

> public diplomacy...litigation public relations aimed at influencing the outcomes of jury trials, public health campaigns, development public relations aimed at building support for national development programs, support for social causes...or to develop support for particular candidates or political policies. Such campaigns can help gain acceptance for a corporation's or industry's apologies, public policy views, or products, and to communicate directly with employees. (Botan & Soto, 1995, p. 23)

Black and Härtel (2002) utilize the term "orientation" to describe the "possible philosophical stances of an organization towards public relations" (p. 13). Orientation will therefore function as what this chapter seeks to articulate: the philosophical and rhetorical theoretical ground on which one can practice effective, appropriate, and ethical public relations.

Public relations is always undertaken as a practice embedded within a specific social, economic, and historical context in the midst of previous encounters, changing relationships, multiple conversations, and competing messages seeking to inform and persuade human behavior, speech, and actions. As Scott M. Cutlip (1995) states, "it is a truism that 'practice should be informed by history'" (p. 279). J. Michael Sproule notes in a 1988 article that the influence of the past on present practice in noting "the shift during the last four generations from oratorical to managerial forms of social control is evident whether one focuses on source, audience, or message" (p. 468). More recently, Stuart Ewen (1996), in commenting on the ambiguities of Edward Bernays's approach to public relations, describes the "murky dissonance separating one who is responding to from one who seeks to manage the public mind—have marked the history of public relations throughout the twentieth century" (p. 400). As these authors suggest, public relations practice seeks to initiate relationships between different parties, a goal that could be greatly augmented by adopting a dialogic meeting approach to more appropriate and effective communication. The idea of two-way communication "is a pivotal element of the ideology of public relations" from its espousal "by Ivy Lee and Edward Bernays early in the century and advocated in professional models of public relations ever since" (Mayhew, 1997, p. 203).

Researchers Grunig and Hunt (1984) identify asymmetrical and symmetrical models of two-way communication. The two-way asymmetrical model of public relations uses scientific research methods to discover how to persuade publics according to the desires of clients. Although Grunig and Hunt describe asymmetrical two-way communication as a "selfish" model ill-suited to conflict resolution (1994, p. 9), they advocate for greater implementation of the two-way symmetrical model of public relations. Symmetrical two-way communication provides an excellent approach to conflict resolution as it seeks to promote mutual understanding among clients and publics. Mayhew (1997) states that "two-way communication requires public relations professionals to represent the public to their client as well as transmitting the client's message to the public" (p. 203). Two-way symmetrical public relations not only describes the work of "excellent departments" but also "produces better long-term relationships with publics...generally are conducted more ethically...and produce effects that balance the interests of organizations and the publics in society" (Grunig, Grunig & Dozier, 2002, p. 15). The dialogic meeting orientation prescribed here seeks to further texture this notion of two-way communication through the articulation of the rich rhetorical and philosophical ideas that can further enhance such communication to generate effective relationships.

A Pragmatic Ethics of Meeting Publics in Dialogue

Such a conception of communication as a process of give-and-take presupposes a process-oriented concept of publics. It also suggests a responsive and active audience theory that posits that audiences themselves play an important part in shaping their interpretations of the messages they receive, sometimes in ways that counter the intention behind the messages articulated by public relations professionals and media sources (Mayhew, 1997). A philosophical and rhetorical approach to public relations grounded in dialogic meeting promotes ethical interaction. As discussed and as Botan (1997) notes, "the ethicality of strategic communication can be analyzed not so much in terms of its content as its process—the relationship it assumes or enforces between the involved parties—and the attitudes and values it reflects" (p. 190). Ethical interaction is promoted by a dialogic meeting orientation because it orders two-way communication to foster the responsive and active responsive participation of each interlocutor grounded in trust and openness.

The ethical components of such an approach and how it shapes how one defines public relations practice is important because it enacts the theory behind the communicative actions. As Beninger and Dordick and others characterize our current historical moment as the information age, one must be attuned to the growing role public relations will play in the lives of organizations (Botan, 1997, p. 192). This accords with Schement's claim that a majority of the workforce will be engaged in such "information work" as strategic communication and public relations (Botan, 1997). Envisioning public relations as information work posits it as "the production, distribution, transformation, storage, retrieval, or use of information" (Paisley, 1994, p. 118). Public relations is an example of information work because it is "part of the emerging information society...because information is the primary tool of strategic communication campaigns, including public relations...Indeed, it is hard to conceive of any endeavor that is more quintessentially information work than is strategic communication" (Botan, 1997, p. 192).

As Bovet (1995) suggests, "[P]ower and productivity in the new order are based on developing and distributing information–two of the primary activities of public relations" (p. 1). This increase in information and information technology emphasizes the necessity of positive relationships between publics and organizations as the chances that a corporate or organizational problematic behavior will not be noticed diminish (Botan, 1997, p. 193).

However, are current paradigms of public relations practice suited to constructively address these changing contexts? Following a review of the literature and work by Grunig and Hunt, Botan (1997) claims that a "technician perspective on public relations [a.k.a., a 'hired gun'] is by far the dominant model of public relations practice and teaching today" (p. 194). An inherent deficit in this approach lies with its abdication of responsibility regarding ethical concerns. In a technician approach, the

> public relations department usually accepts what is essentially a one-way communication role and assures it will have little voice in deciding what is ethical for the organization to do with respect to its publics or in deciding exactly how public relations will be practiced. In fact those making the calls under this model are often organizational leaders with little or no training in communication, in communication campaigns, in persuasion, or in the media and its role in society. They often do not even have basic training in the legal or ethical aspects of public communication campaigns. (Botan, 1997, p. 195)

Such an orientation employs a monologic approach to communication and public relations. The poverty of this perspective resides in its tendency to instrumentalize people and publics not as partners in discourse and relationships but as tools to be manipulated to meet the unquestioned ends of the client. People and publics are viewed as mere malleable masses, "site[s] where the speaker seeks to meet his/her needs" (Botan, 1997, p. 195) denying the dynamic qualities inherent in both people and publics.

A "hired gun" orientation to public relations raises not only ethical but practical questions as well. How could one sustain any productive long-term relationships with publics employing a monologic approach especially given the current context of the information age in which we reside where messages are mediated and analyzed through multiple sources by multiple publics regarded of the intended aim of a monologic approach? One-way communication or a monologic orientation to public relations falsifies the true nature of how communication occurs in reality, and risks reifying people and publics into means and tools of unquestioned corporate or organizational ends. Such practices seem a shade closer to the borders of state-run propaganda rather than the professional practice of public relations. Inherent problems with the present model call for alternative approaches, to which this discussion seeks to respond.

A constructive approach to public relations grounded in a dialogic meeting orientation shifts "the emphasis in public relations from managing publics and public opinion to a new emphasis on building, nurturing and maintaining relationships" (Ledingham & Brunig qtd. in Kent & Taylor, 2002, p. 23). This move toward looking at dialogue as offering a new, constructive orientation to public relations originated with Robert Pearson's work, "A Theory of Public Relations Ethics." Pearson's (1989) comments on the ethical advantages emanating from such a change in orientation strongly reinforce the approach advocated here:

> If what is right and wrong in organization conduct cannot be intuited or arrived at by some monological process, as much postmodern theory and postmodern philosophy in general argues, then the focus for an organizational ethicist must shift dramatically. The important question becomes, not what action or policy is more right than another (a question that is usually posed as a monologue), but what kind of communication system maximizes the chances competing interests can discover some shared ground and be transformed or transcended. This question shifts the em-

phasis from an area in which practitioners do not have special expertise-
ethical theory–to areas in which they do have expertise–communication
theory and practice. (p. 206)

Such a shift in emphasis has implications not only for the orientation and practices of public relations professionals but also re-
invests how they approach the different parties with which they
interact.

Organizations are cast in a new light by a shift to a dialogic
meeting orientation to information work. As Pearson (1989) stated,
for organizations have a moral imperative to "establish and maintain communication relationships with all publics affected by organizational action and, by implication, morally wrong not to do so"
(p. 329). Michael A. Kent and Maureen Taylor (2002) continue with
this theme, adding that what "dialogue does is change the nature
of the organization-public relationship by placing emphasis on the
relationship" (p. 24). Placing greater emphasis on the conversation
between the organization and the public, on the communicative and
real relationship they share, emphasizes the dual social and economic nature of organizations as public entities. Ewen (1996) notes
that such a change emerged in the twentieth century as a result
of drastically altered social and economic states in response to the
Great Depression and the advent of welfare capitalism.

Robert Wood Johnson, writing while serving as the head of
Johnson & Johnson pharmaceutical company, stressed in 1949 that
"business must develop a 'permanent and complete social policy'. It
must assume a position of social 'trusteeship', as he put it, to attune
its interests to those of the general public" (Johnson as qtd. in Ewen,
1996, p. 362). Given our current historical moment of enhanced media technology spreading messages and organizational information
to widely diverse audiences, merely magnifies the rhetorical advantage of adapting and reapplying Johnson's sage counsel. Johnson
suggested that "[t]rusteeship would emphasize our points of common interests and responsibility, not merely our differences. Such a
spirit would bring new health to the business world. It would over-
flow into political life, with patriotism and concern for the common
good mitigating struggles by pressure groups and special interests"
(as qtd. in Ewen, 1996, p. 527). A dialogic meeting orientation to
information work emphasizes the ethical and rhetorical necessity
of such a position for an organization to engage publics in communication and foster relationships built on trust. Given our current

American corporate climate splintered and blackened by the poisonous odor of eminent scandal since the Enron and dot.com disasters, reseeing organizations as responsible social and economic institutions seems highly advantageous.

A textured understanding of publics or the public sphere, which organizations seek to engage through the information work of public relations professionals, depends on a related reorientation to the idea of the public. A public is viewed as constituted of *"the interdependent members of society who hold different opinions about a mutual problem and who seek to influence its resolution through discourse"*; developed societies can therefore be understood as "montages" of such publics (Hauser, 1999, p. 32). It is important to be cognizant of the dynamic nature of publics and their discourses. Publics are not pregiven; publics emerge; "any given public exists in its publicness, in its rhetorical character" (Hauser, 1999, p. 33). Hauser's insights into this multifaceted metaphor also inform the related ideas of a public sphere.

A Dialogic Rhetoric of Judgment

According to Hauser (1999) a public sphere will be "defined as a *discursive space in which individuals and groups associate to discuss matters of mutual interest and, where possible, to reach a common judgment about them*" (p. 61). This describes the setting in which organizations and publics engage in conversation and develop relationships. It assumes that publics are defined by their actions, not reflections, that is, "that publics only [develop] as they manifest their publicness" (Hauser, 1999, p. 97). This standpoint presupposes three main underlying ideas. First, "publics do not exist as entities but as processes; their collective reasoning is not defined by abstract reflection but by practical judgment; their awareness of issues is not philosophical but eventful" (Hauser, 1999, p. 64). Second, a "public's emergence is not dependent on consensus but on the sharing of a common world, even when understood and lived differently by different segments of society" (Hauser, 1999, p. 69). Such a conception implies that the "public engages in contesting and creating meaning" (Mayhew, 1997, p. 5), not in a priori Pavlovian response to prefabricated sources of stimuli and influence. Treated in this manner, publics are dynamic processes that must be engaged, not static entities that must be manipulated according to persistent techniques. A third and related notion is that a public's nature is not solely determined by its shared interests but "rested upon their community, rested on the rhetorical experience of sharing a public relationship of words and deeds" (Hauser, 1999, p. 60). The "communicative environment conditions our publicness" (Hauser, 1999, p. 60) and influences the judgments that we reach as members of different publics.

The conception of judgment as a civil activity forms the ground of such a concept of a public or publicness although presupposing public opinion as the expression of the particular public considered (Hauser, 1999). As previously stated, publics are defined by judgment (Hauser, 1999). The notion of judgment as the defining act and element of publics emphasizes the rhetorical elements of the alternative constructive approach to public relations sketched through this conversation. "Civil judgments reflect a common understanding that not only expresses a rhetorically formed public opinion but is the very ground for a public" (Hauser, 1999, p. 98). This does not presuppose a static conception of judgment as a calcified event that retains a set element of significance. Rather, judgment *"is a form of knowledge constituted by the very performance and appraisal of discourse in terms of the world our collective activity promises to frame"* (Hauser, 1999, p. 100). Information workers possess great ability to influence given their access to and dissemination of information and their appeals to various audiences through the multiple venues technology makes available.

Hauser makes explicit the rhetorical element of judgment, tracing the idea back to Aristotle's treatise, *On Rhetoric*. Hauser (1999) demonstrates that Aristotle's views on the role of judgment in discourse "are relevant...insofar as they offer insight in to the type of reasoning peculiar to public life" (p. 98). As Hauser (1999) explains, the idea of krisis or judgment implies:

> More than rational ascent; it is a virtue of judgment informed by a disposition to act and feel in a particular way. The rationality of krisis entails the virtue of considering the phenomena of prudential conduct in terms that exceed one's personal interests and apply to every human. Krisis is not exercised as a calculus of consequences but as a thoughtful consideration of contingent affairs in order to achieve the common good of *eudaimonia*, or happiness. (p. 98)

Repositioning the act of judgment as central to the communication of a public's opinion also repositions "discourse at the center of *public* opinion" that provides a wealth of opportunities for "divulging public opinion, understanding its formation, and interpreting its meaning" (Hauser, 1999, p. 85). It also centers "society's ongoing conversation within the domain of forming and expressing public opinion" that "refocuses attention on praxis, at once more complex and more faithful to the practices of actors themselves" (Hauser, 1999, p. 85). Meeting publics in dialogue affords a coconstructive orientation to interpretation and judgment. The praxis of joining in the communicative space opened by a dialogic orientation to ideas and events helps to construct a bridge between dialogue and rhetoric. Links between communication, interpretation, and judgment will offer an opportunity for rhetoric to enable coconstruction of meaning between organizations and publics in an open and honest way to lasting and mutually beneficial relationships.

Implications for Public Relations Praxis

Rhetoric therefore functions within this conception of a public and public opinion as "a means of entering public life. Rhetoric integrates culture and eloquence by providing life-enhancing vocabularies for active social participation" (Mayhew, 1997, p. 35). Rhetorical appeals undertaken by information workers to sway the opinion of a public urge a convergence of the interests of organization and public. Rhetoric moves beyond the scientistic language puzzles and hazy numerical Gordian knots of experts to employing reason and eloquence to move. As Mayhew (1997) notes, building on John Dewey's comments regarding the art of presentation, only the "incorporation of the eloquence of rhetoric into discourses of public life will furnish persuasive appeal to reasonable argument" (p. 47). Botan and Soto (1995) reemphasize this notion through their claim that "any communicative activity on the part of a public is, a priori, rhetorical" (p. 41). This dynamic conception of the malleable nature of the creation and persuasion of public opinion reveals the dialogic character of this rhetorical exchange. "Because of the requisites of persuasion, in practice, reason takes the form of rhetorical rebuttal of rhetorical statement. Reason can only be realized in dialogue" (Mayhew, 1997, p. 48) and dialogue can best be fostered through an approach that is constructive and cognizant of the philosophical, historical, rhetorical, and ethical elements of public relations practice.

In conclusion, a constructive rhetorical orientation to public relations practice engages dialogic meeting to inform, influence, and enrich relationships between organizations and publics. These dialogic meetings also enable communication between parties to ethically, appropriately, and effectively energize responses from multiple and diverse parties to a dialogue they had not been able to hear and respond to previously. Granted the costs would be high, yet the yield could bring continually growing returns rooted firmly in the ground of trust between parties to the dialogue. Parties are encouraged to actively listen, engage, and respond to the messages that flow in multiple directions and activate threads of other conversations simultaneously occurring, thus providing ethically rich and multifarious opportunities to inform, influence, and enrich not only contemporary but also future public relations practice between diverse parties in our postmodern moment.

An orientation to public relations practice grounded in a rhetorical, philosophical dialogic meeting orientation works out of and in response to the current historical moment. Such an orientation seeks to nurture and enrich communicative actions and relationships between organizations and publics. This would avoid dictatorial, blind, and deaf technique-driven application of static communicative actions to a multitude of contexts, often resulting in counterproductive and monologic public relations failures and crises.

Ignorance of the historical context and the other ongoing conversations that influence how public relations practice and messages are received by various diverse publics risk one persuading more often by chance than by art (Lewis, 1996, p. 21). Ambiguity or lack of awareness of the reasons why one pursues the ends he or she does can have grave consequences for one whose work is the establishment and nurturing of relationships through discourse. Public relations practice aware of and responsive to the historical moment aids constructive communication and heightens the possibilities for dialogic and multilogic interactions to emerge and enrich the relationships between organizations and publics.

References

Aristotle. (1991). *On rhetoric: A theory of civic discourse.* (G. A. Kennedy, Trans.). Oxford: Oxford University Press.

Arnett, R. C., & Arneson, P. (1999). *Dialogic civility in a cynical age: Community, hope, and interpersonal relationships.* Albany: State University of New York Press.

Bakhtin, M. M. (1984). *Problems of Dostoevsky's poetics.* (C. Emerson, Ed. & Trans.). Minneapolis: University of Minnesota Press.

———. (1986). *Speech genres and other late essays.* (V. W. McGee, Trans., C. Emerson & M. Holquist, Eds.). Austin: University of Texas Press.

———. (1991). *The dialogic imagination: Four essays.* (M. Holquist & C. Emerson, Trans., M. Holquist, Ed.). Austin: University of Texas Press.

Black, L., & Härtel, C. E. J. (2002). Towards a typology of the public relations behavior of organizations. *Journal of Business Communication,* 39, 11-19.

Botan, C. H. (1997). Ethics in strategic communication campaigns: The case for a new approach to public relations. *Journal of Business Communication,* 34, 187-201.

Botan, C. H., & Soto, F. (1995). A semiotic approach to the internal functioning of publics: Implications for strategic communication and public relations. *Public Relations Review,* 24, 21-44.

Bovet, S. F. (1995). Public relations can dominate new era. *Public Relations Journal,* 51, 1-5.

Cutlip, S. M. (1995). *Public relations history: From the 17th to the 20th century.* The antecedents. Hillsdale, NJ: Lawrence Erlbaum.

Ewen, S. (1996). *PR! A social history of spin.* New York: Basic Books.

Grunig, J., & Hunt, T. (1984). *Managing public relations.* New York: Holt, Rinehart & Winston.

———. (1994). *Public relations techniques.* Fort Worth, TX: Harcourt Brace College.

Grunig, L., Grunig, J., & Dozier, D. (2002). *Excellent public relations and effective organizations: A study of communication management in three countries.* Mahwah, NJ: Lawrence Erlbaum.

Hauser, G. A. (1999). *Vernacular voices: The rhetoric of publics and public spheres.* Columbia: University of South Carolina Press.

Holquist, M. (1990). *Dialogism: Bakhtin and his world.* New York: Routledge.

Johnson, R. W. (1949). Human relations in modern business. *Harvard Business Review,* 27, 521-541.

Kent, M. A., & Taylor, M. (2002). Toward a dialogic theory of public relations. *Public Relations Review,* 28, 21-37.

Lewis, C. S. (1996). *The abolition of man.* New York: Touchstone.

Mayhew, L. H. (1997). *The new public: Professional communication and the means of social influence.* Cambridge: Cambridge University Press.

Paisley, W. (1994). Information and work. In B. Dervin & M. Voight (Eds.), *Progress in communication sciences* (pp. 113-166). Norwood, NJ: Ablex.

Pearson, R. (1989). A theory of public relations ethics. Unpublished doctoral dissertation, Ohio University.

Sproule, J. M. (1988). The new managerial rhetoric and the old criticism. *Quarterly Journal of Speech,* 74, 468-486.

Vice, S. (1997). *Introducing Bakhtin.* New York: St. Martin's Press.

Chapter 6

Narrative Literacy: A Communicative Practice of Interpretation for the Ethical Deliberation of Contentious Organizational Narratives

Elesha L. Ruminski

It can be unnerving or even frightening when others misunderstand our communication because they know little to nothing about us or the lives and organizations in which we are embedded. Sensing a lack of historical perspective about organizational narratives can be demoralizing, especially within any organization that has weathered intense political change. Within such contentious settings, opportunities to find common ground or create a shared organizational narrative can be lost unless organizational members, as communicators, are willing participants eager to learn about others. Embracing a communicative approach that promotes continuous learning within organizations takes more than trying to understand being in someone else's shoes; rather, learning about the Other's experience in the world to gain understanding of the person's narrative(s)[1] would be more beneficial. In other words, it would be helpful to better understand not only individual standpoints but additionally the socially constructed narrative(s) in which people are embedded. Engaging in an ongoing communicative process of interpretation of organizational narrative(s) can help us understand different forms of sensemaking and coalition-building that are contributing to an organization's narrative contention.

To examine this important organizational communication approach, this chapter explores application of narrative literacy, a uniquely identified kind of literacy that functions as a communicative practice of interpretation that enables ethical communicative responses.[2] The metaphor of narrative literacy is revealed through a scholarly intersection that emphasizes how critically conscious reading of organizational narratives framed by an ethic Ronald C. Arnett and Pat Arneson (1999) refer to as "dialogic civility" can reinforce what Arnett (2001) calls "a pragmatic commitment to keeping the conversation going in a time of narrative confusion and virtue fragmentation" (p. 315). Built on a communication perspective of narrative following Walter Fisher's lead and Paulo Freire and Donald Macedo's (1987) premise that *literacy* requires liberation, narrative literacy can assist us in tolerating decreased certainty within various interpersonal and organizational contexts, a requirement for communicating ethically in a postmodern time.

A note of caution here: Liberation is not to be perceived as a breaking free from everything; it is not just a radical overture. Instead, liberation should be understood to be a requirement of being a free thinker engaged in perceptive, constructive, flexible participation within an organizational context. Specifically, as this chapter demonstrates, narrative literacy can enhance the ethical invitation, reception, and even rejection of various narrative perspectives within a particular labor organization, the International Brotherhood of Teamsters (IBT). Labor unions are known to deal with organizational narrative contention, so awareness of narrative conflicts in this particular organizational context is essential to ethical, inclusive communication.

So what is the significance of discussing this type of communication ethics-oriented literacy within an organizational setting? Narrative literacy might assist us in tolerating increased ambiguity, a requirement for communicating ethically in a postmodern time. Postmodernity is characterized by Arnett and Arneson (1999) as a time of "metanarrative disruption in which common sense is rarer simply because we have fewer common experiences" (p. 54). Since we must acknowledge that multiple narratives exist in postmodernity, we cannot assume very much about shared values; therefore, we must become critical *readers* of the moral constructs guiding others as we encounter others–each time we encounter others. Narrative literacy is therefore an important metaphor to consider because of our need to remain ethical as we confront the Other within a variety of contexts, particularly professional environments where the interpersonal differences might be superseded for organizational purposes.

Arnett and Arneson (1999) highlight that both Hans-Georg Gadamer (1976) and Paulo Freire (2002) point to a *reading* metaphor, and they suggest that "dialogue accepts a person as a text that needs to be opened up" (p. 185). Thus reading offers a rich analogy for communication studies because it emphasizes perception and interpretation as well as imagination. Readers of literature often make meaning of "texts" in discursive fashion, revising their understanding as they read, as new text emerges, or as new circumstances framing the reading materialize. Similarly, we might hope to "read" as we communicate with others, recognizing that the lives of others involve layered "living texts" with continuously changing circumstances, even in the most conservative of organizational contexts. As Arnett (2002) explains, we will overlook the person if we don't contextualize his or her place in the world.

To gain a better understanding of how narrative literacy can be a useful process for ethical communication within organizations, use of the terms "narrative" and "literacy" will first be clarified and the emergence of the pairing of these terms as a single communication metaphor will be traced. Next, narrative literacy will be compared to a similar term of E.D. Hirsch, Joseph F. Kett, and James Trefil's (2002) *cultural literacy* to reveal the significant distinction in embracing narrative literacy from a communication perspective. Then, an example of organizational narrative contention will be detailed: an overview of the competing narrative perspectives evident within the IBT during the deliberation of the organization's title in 1996 will be the special case examined here. Finally, pragmatic considerations will be offered, with discussion of how narrative literacy is distinguished from standpoint theory and how various standpoints can be better invited, received, or even rejected as contextually and ethically appropriate through narrative literacy.

Narrative as a Communicative Metaphor and Moral Construct

The term narrative has different meanings depending on disciplinary use. In literary studies, narrative is commonly understood to indicate a story or plotline. In composition studies, it is a rhetorical mode of writing that uses the first person to tell a story of one's experiences and feelings. Here, in a study of organizational communication, the term narrative draws on Arnett's definition: He says narrative is "a background set of tacit assumptions and knowledge about communication that guide and offer meaning to the foreground event of a given conversation" (Arnett qtd. in Arnett & Arneson, 1999, p. 57). This view builds on Walter R. Fisher's (2000) definition of the narrative paradigm; Fisher says, "Narratives begin as a speech act, take the form of a story, and when people begin to be collectively guided by a given story, a narrative [or a 'communication background'] is given birth" (p. 304). Fisher affirms, "Narratives are moral constructs" (p. 300) and states, "The narrative paradigm...can be considered a dialectical synthesis of two traditional strands in the history of rhetoric: the argumentative, persuasive theme and the literary, aesthetic theme" (p. 291). Fisher's (2000) narrative paradigm relies on Kenneth Burke's definition of humans as "symbol using animals" (p. 296). This reflects Freire's (2002) view of pedagogy, which assists people, as "language animals" in developing generative metaphors. Thus, narrative offers a rich metaphor for a collective organizational story as it points to the interpretive act of reading.

Arnett and Arneson (1999) suggest that narrative is teleological, culturally learned, and evidenced in "everyday practice" (p. 58, 62). They suggest, "Narrative points to a why prior to engaging in communication together" (p. 60). Narratives are enthymemes, rhetorical syllogisms (Aristotle, 2004), that have buy in and "collective power" that resist ideology (pp. 19, 21-22). This is because narratives aren't prescribed or forced upon others; they are instead emergent because people participate in and create narratives together through learning (Arnett, 2002). Therefore, it is appropriate that Arnett and Arneson's (1999) dialogic civility offers a public narrative background that "has a baseline of respect for others as human beings" (p. 55) and the "narrative requirements of participation, phronesis, and genuine listening to the particular historical moment" (p. 57). If our task is "to build new public narratives that can bind us together" (p. 60), narrative literacy can be helpful in learning how to communicate in the midst of the existence of multiple narratives or various perspectives on shared narratives. The focus of this approach orients organizational participants toward the locating of mutual ethics that inform the particular differing, often contentious, narratives we work from and encounter. That process of locating these shared ethics through continuous learning is evident through the term "literacy."

Positioning Literacy as a Liberating Communicative Act

Narrative literacy relies on the view of literacy as social and cultural construct and springs from a similar metaphor, Laurie Moroco and Kathleen Roberts' (2002) *narrative fluency.*[3] Their discussion of narrative fluency responded to the need to have "a repertoire of many languages, and to recognize the various registers within a linguistic community as not deficient, but different" (p. 5). They cite Alasdair MacIntyre in suggesting, "The narrative of any one life is part of an interlocking set of narratives." Therefore, in discussing African American discourse as an example, they claim, "Ethically, in recognizing our own story as interlocked with those of other people, it is our responsibility to hear their story as well—to attain *narrative fluency.* Thus, the goal is to become fluent in the narrative of African America—through its vernacular discourse" (Moroco & Roberts, 2002, pp. 7-8).

Fluency is defined by *Oxford Dictionary of Current English* as "flowing naturally" or "verbally facile, especially in a foreign language." Although the premise of narrative fluency is reasonable, fluency might be an overly rigorous assessment of ethical responsibility in a postmodern time. Rather, literacy, following Freire's view of the term, might frame the ethic of inter- and intra-narrative communication in a problem-posing, pedagogical way that works from the view that learning is never finished. Thus, narrative literacy is a constructive interpretive extension of narrative fluency.[4] Arnett (2002) has already suggested that literacy is imperative for communication. He proposes that relying upon a communication ethic that is learning-focused and story-centered will create a story about literacy itself that empowers others and increases their capability to engage in organizations.

The definition of literacy has been greatly debated. The debate involves whether literacy should be viewed as a skill, a knowledge, or what James Potter calls "a perspective on the world" (Christ & Potter, 2002, p. 5). This third view, *literacy as social and cultural construct,* was initiated in the 1960s by critical theorists including Antonio Gramsci, Henry Giroux, and Paulo Freire. Literacy as an act of consciousness provides a "becoming of awareness" aimed at reconstructing a public and democratic life (Willis, 1997). Septima Clark's citizenship classes, the Freedom Riders, the rise of ethnic and gender studies in universities, and the implementation of affirmative action show how literacy as praxis mingled with activism, education, and institutions in previous historical moments (Willis, 1997).

Freire defines literacy as a strategy of liberation that teaches people to "read the word and the world" (qtd. in Willis, 1997). Freire considers a banking model of education as dichotomizing, depositing, top-down transaction of ideas as things, when students passively memorize and regurgitate imposed answers as "knowledge." He says, "Words are emptied of their concreteness and become a hollow, alienated, and alienating verbosity" (p. 71) in banking style literacy. Rather, with his reliance on "lived experience," Freire views literacy as dialogic and focuses on "saving face to the public requirements of a historical situation, not private psychological need" (Arnett & Arneson, 1999, p. 187). Literacy to Freire is twofold: reading texts as well as understanding the standpoint or politics of what is read to better understand deep structural meaning and participate better in institutions (Arnett, 2002). Therefore, Freire's theory of literacy is applicable to a textured understanding of organizational communication because it calls for a dual interpretive accountability.

Distinguishing Narrative Literacy
from Cultural Literacy

An important distinction to make is between narrative literacy and another similar scholarly term, cultural literacy. *The Dictionary of Cultural Literacy* by E. D. Hirsch, Jr., Joseph F. Kett, and James Trefil (2002) provides what the authors identify as "necessary knowledge" for Americans. The authors define cultural literacy as "the context of what we say and read; it is part of what makes Americans American" (2002, p. x). More than 6,000 entries "concisely sum up the knowledge that matters to Americans" (jacket cover). Hirsch says in the third-edition preface, "I say 'to Americans' because the concept of cultural literacy implies a national culture" (p. vii). As a disclaimer, Hirsch suggests that these definitions might prompt debates among Americans, which indicates multiple narratives could vie for input into what constitutes the American narrative or American cultural literacy of the time.

Cultural literacy seems to be striving for agreement on an overarching narrative of American cultural knowledge that is easily digestible and publishable. Alternatively, narrative literacy acknowledges that the ethical intersection of multiple narratives or multiple perspectives of a shared narrative requires lived experience and continuous learning that acknowledges historical circumstances. This is because Freire's view of literacy is the pedagogy of the oppressed, which confronts the power of political and organizational structures with learning about multiple narratives (Arnett, 2002). Yet narrative literacy moves beyond cultural terminology about the American narrative to the free-flowing, symbolic narratives of life. Narrative literacy helps organizational communicators recognize that not everyone shares the same perspective of a particular organizational narrative let alone the same particular organizational narrative, as the following example illustrates. As an interpretive, communicative approach, narrative literacy can assist organizational participants as they negotiate organizational narrative meanings, allowing alternative perspectives and narratives to coexist as necessary as they navigate change.

Teamsters Narrative Contention: The Name Change Debate

The IBT, which is one of the largest U.S. based labor unions, celebrated a century of existence in 2003. Robert D. Leiter (1974) says, "Teamsters are employed to move goods from one place to another and in that role have played an important role in the economic development of the United States" (p. 15). United Parcel Service composes the largest percentage of Teamsters. Today, Teamster truckers, warehouse workers, nurses, communication specialists, and members in many other fields are among the minority of workers who continue to engage in collective bargaining in the United States.

According to the IBT Strategic Planning Committee of 2000, "'Teamsters' ... is a term with its own its meaning of a labor union that is the largest and most powerful in the world" (p. 5). Teamsters are some of the most recognizable of union members because, as IBT Communications Director Brett Caldwell (personal communication, 2004) suggests, members identify themselves strongly as Teamsters and consider themselves members of a brotherhood. Labor organizations use the term "brotherhood" to communicate their sense of community and shared values. Brotherhood in this context situates a group as affiliated with a particular work ethic that acknowledges the members' connection and dedication to a particular community. Traditionally, the IBT reflected a fraternity of blue-collar workers bound through a shared sense of Teamsters history and likely the fact that family members before them had been members too. As a brotherhood, IBT members rhetorically separated themselves from those who were not working-class members, which would include in particular those in management or politicians who are not labor-friendly.

Brotherhood has been defined secularly and religiously to indicate a blood relationship or close familial bond between people, regardless of gender. Plato, who once wrote that women were equal to men in the state, claimed one's fellow citizen was a brother, while Xenophon considered a friend a brother (Agonito, 1977; Ratzinger, 1996). Although religious doctrine typically espouses a paternal view by considering brotherhood a reference to all of God's children, Enlightenment natural rights doctrine indicates that brotherhood means the call to bring all humans to natural equality (Ratzinger, 1996). In the Marxist idea of fraternity, two ethical zones arise to separate those who are brothers (the proletariat) from those who are not (the bourgeois). Most references to brotherhood recognize that an outsider can become a brother only through initiation. Some groups have historically used the term "sister" analogously to indicate what brother means. However, sisterhood has also been defined by second-wave feminists to mean the identifiable social consciousness of the women's movement (Donovan, 2000).

Thus, the organizational narrative that many Teamsters embrace is synonymous with belonging to and serving a brotherhood. The narrative contention that arose, then, came when the concept of the brotherhood became a topic of deliberation during the Teamsters 1996 annual international convention. Teamster members who believed the time had come to change the image of the union took the convention floor to make their case. Rather than be identified as the International *Brotherhood* of Teamsters, several members, both women and men, lobbied for a new name: the *Teamsters International Union*. By changing this language in the union's name to remove the term *brotherhood*, the hope was that the IBT would be viewed as more inclusive of women, thus creating a more invitational organizational narrative. Although serving as a deliberation of the gendered language of the union, the name change debate was also a heated political debate between the two primary slates running for election that year. In the midst of a highly emotional debate, two visions of how to invite and accommodate women members arose: one group wanted to change the title of the organization by eliminating the term brotherhood, thus emphasizing a new external image of the IBT that projected updated organizational savvy and gender sensitivity; and another vision to keep the same name, thus retaining a traditional narrative perspective that also saved money and resisted undue political fervor over a gender issue within the union.

These two groups could be said to represent divergent organizational narratives or at least two distinct perspectives of the emergent Teamster narrative at the turn of the twenty-first century. Primarily, the two competing views of the organizational narrative broke down between members affiliated with the more liberal, grassroots reform group Teamsters for a Democratic Union (TDU) and the TDU-backed Carey/Kilmury administration, which was in office at the time, who supported the name change to remove brotherhood references; and the more conservative, old-guard affiliated Hoffa/Hogan slate, which promoted that the union's name be left intact to continue the brotherhood narrative. The Hoffa camp referred to those who proposed the name change as dissenters, but these "dissenters" considered themselves activists for the rank and file and the unorganized, suggesting that a name change would help the union modernize to stay current with changing labor force dynamics. As IBT Legislative and Political Action Committee Co-chairperson Joe Padellaro suggested, as indicated in the 1996 IBT convention proceedings, the change would "make it clear that this union is a union for everyone" (p. 355).

On the basis of a historical call to reinvigorate the labor movement by organizing women members, the proposal for name change came forth primarily from women delegates from Local 2000 in Bloomington, Minnesota, a local of flight attendants with 8,000 female members and 2,000 male members. With interruptions from the convention floor, Delegate Anne Toombs suggested that the new name, *Teamsters International Union*, was desirable:

> The name is simple. Keeps the word "International," because we have members in two countries, the U.S. and Canada. It says we're all Teamsters without leaving out the hundreds of thousands of members who are women, like the word brotherhood does. Most importantly, it puts the magic word right up front, Teamsters. (p. 355)

Clearly, the group's intent was to promote an international status and public identification with the term "Teamster" in a more progressive light that would suggest that the union promoted gender equity by removing what was perceived to be too gender-specific a term, brotherhood. Their argument was that the name of the organization needed to adapt to the times to be more open to women in unions, which reflects how this particular group of organizational members preferred to promote a moral construct of gender inclusiveness. Thus, the Teamster organizational narrative was considered stagnant and in need of ethical revision by some.

Proponents of the name change identified past name changes: In 1908, "helpers" was added to include a broader definition of Teamsters. In 1910, "chauffeur and stablemen" were added, and in 1940 "stablemen" was dropped and "warehousemen" was added. In these cases, the specific work role references changed as the representation of the majority of members changed (IBT, 1996, p. 357). In 2000, "the proud tradition of being a Teamster" was reinforced by a successful proposal to modernize the name IBT, chauffeurs, and warehousemen of America to simply IBT, which would account for all the trades and industries represented as well as the fact that 100,000 Canadians were members (IBT Strategic Planning Committee, 2000, p. 5). Thus, the image evolved from considering Teamsters as men with horse-drawn teams to a broader generic understanding of what Teamsters might do, yet many thought that this understanding still implied Teamsters were men congregating in a brotherhood.

Members who wanted the new name change argued that women should be welcomed into a union, not a brotherhood, for several reasons: (1) change is good, (2) changing labor demographics suggested the need to organize more women, and (3) women expected equal rights since they live in a country in which the Nineteenth Amendment was added long ago (IBT, 1996, p. 357). One delegate evoked the comparison of women's opportunities in the Teamsters to African American rights in the civil rights movement, while another pleaded,

> I ask for your support to reach out to the growing segment of the labor force, organizing women, working women, so that we as a union may grow together. With your help and support, we can bring inclusion to all, everybody, not just the men, not just truck drivers, everyone. (p. 358)

Another member, Delegate Pauline Woodson of Local 237 in

New York, addressed how a name change was in line with a new approach to organizing, necessary to curb declining membership numbers that were part of the economic trends of the 1990s:

> Changing the name of our union, the International Union, strengthens our union by laying a foundation for future organizational drives. It sends a message to members that our union encourages brothers and sisters alike to participate in union activities. It sends a message that our union fights for working men and women alike. This is the 1990s. Women are a major part of our union and a major part of our workforce that we're trying to organize ... Changing to a name that's all-inclusive will help us to organize. (p. 363)

Similarly, Delegate Linda Cotham of Local 743 in Chicago called for the IBT to get with the times, again echoing, "This is the 1990s. Women are in positions of power in Congress and throughout the state and local government. It's going to help us to have a name that is in touch with the 1990s" (IBT, 1996, p. 366).

Vice President Diane Kilmury, part of the Carey slate and an early activist of the TDU movement, took a progressive and severe stance about the fate of the union's future in respect to its image:

> I'm standing on the beach of this union staring into the future. First off, I've got to kick all the red herrings from underneath my feet. I suppose all the people that are very worried about the expense of changing a logo or a name are not very conversant with computers. But as I look up their speech, I see a raging sea. That raging sea is the employer fighting against us, using everything that they know how to, to divide, be it race, be it our religion, be it our nationality, to divide us from one so that we can be conquered. And in the next century, are we going to be the only international union rowing backwards? When you go through a raging sea, folks, you put the prow to the front and you row forwards. (p. 369)

Delegate Gloria Johnson (personal communication, January 2003) of Local 237 in New York, also president of the Civil Service Bar Association representing a sector of attorneys in New York, said that many professional members felt excluded because of the current name. Some women reacted to the sexism they had experienced in the union:

"[S]ome of my brothers here prefer to refer to women by anatomical body parts. My name is Kim. You will call me so. And I am your sister, I am not your brother" (IBT, 1996, p. 369-370). This delegate, Kim Shanahan of Local 856 in San Francisco, told the membership about her awkward discussion with her ten-year-old daughter when she was asked, "Mom, why is your union called *brotherhood?*"

Some members strove for narrative consistency by attempting to present a compromise: keep the gender-specific term brotherhood, just add the corresponding female term *sisterhood*. But most delegates implied that the tradition to address each other as "brothers and sisters" needed grounding through the identification of the union as a brotherhood. To them, this term referred to a bond similar to that of a family, a bond stronger than simple workplace unity because a humanized community beyond the workplace was created. Hoffa supporters preferred this philosophy, suggesting the name change proposal was politically motivated and that it would be a wasteful expense. Delegates emphasized frugality as well because, as they claimed, the name change would involve an "astronomical expenditure" of at least "10 million dollars" (pp. 362-363). Delegate Jack Mandaro of Local 95 in Williamsburg, Virginia, suggested that the Carey slate was hypocritical for wanting a name change although it had not specifically invited the International Teamsters Women's Caucus (ITWC), Black Caucus, and retirees to the convention (p. 367).

Delegate Jerry McCown of Local 577 in Amarillo, Texas, proved to have the most effective point in this narrative contention. He pointed out that tradition should prevail because of language conventions—since the annual convention was being held in the City of *Brotherly* Love, Philadelphia: "You don't see nobody from here trying to call [Philadelphia] sisterly love" (IBT, 1996, p. 359). By making a connection with the birthplace of the U.S. Constitution, McCown, even with improper grammar, effectively connected the Teamsters title and the Teamsters organizational narrative to an American ideal of unity.[5]

Although the deliberation of the name change was to promote women's invitation and reception into the IBT, the proposal was met with resistance from many women. Many spoke up to suggest that they did not feel alienated within a brotherhood. Instead, they focused on their pride to be Teamsters with such zeal and emphasized the necessity to retain the current name for tradition's sake that those supporting the name change were left sounding like radical feminists. To support the idea of brotherhood, Delegate Shirley Russell of Local 886 in Oklahoma City, relied on a contradictory, Christian-based argument that suggested we are all part of one humanity, regardless of language conventions:

> The word "brotherhood" to me signifies not gender but unity. (Applause)
> Sisters, we as women should not feel segregated nor made to feel less than
> a part of this union because of the word "brotherhood." Webster defines
> brotherhood as a whole or complete body engaged in a business or profes-
> sion, an association, such as a labor union, for a particular purpose. Just
> like God took the rib from Adam to make Eve, he took that to make him
> complete. (p. 365)

Then, Russell went on to be frank about her view of gender roles, which were based on notions of compulsory heterosexuality and traditional gender stereotypes:

> Men: We as women, we nag you, we mother you, we smother you, and
> we love you. Women: Men, they, in turn, love us, they spoil us, they take
> care of us. Together we have purpose. We are complete. So don't be misled
> by the word "brotherhood" as used in our name. It makes us complete, it
> makes us whole, we have a purpose. (p. 365)

Although Russell seemingly contradicted herself by first saying that members should vote with their heads, not their hearts, and then ending her remarks with "I love you," she proved that narratives involve what Fisher suggests: both persuasion and aesthetic appeal (p. 291).

Delegate Mark Rogstad of Local 524 in Yakima, Washington, spoke up to confirm women's acceptance as Teamsters: "I consider the people in front of me to be Teamsters; I consider the people behind me to be Teamsters, whether they are male or female" (IBT, 1996, p. 359). Delegate Don Thornsburg of Local 986 in Los Angeles suggested the significance of the Teamsters name: "It is not a generic name. It is not a name that can be changed to win votes for you and your delegates. It's a name that will be passed on to my children and my family. I'm proud to be a Teamster." Emotional rather than logical arguments like these represent the unshakeable vision that Teamsters should always be recognized as a brotherhood; by claiming the name is not generic, this member seems to suggest that there is an inherent gender bias implied by the term Teamsters that cannot be sacrificed; however, the term brotherhood is not directly addressed by this delegate. Instead, he reveals his true political intention, exhibiting the passionate politics of period in the union: "We're not here to change the name of the International Union, we're here to change the administration, we're here to change you, you, to put Hoffa where you are, where you are. How long have you destroyed this union?" (IBT, 1996, p. 360).

Many of the speakers tried to separate the issue from the partisan politics. A male delegate raised the point that he felt pride as a Teamster regardless of what the formal name is, commenting that he still has a button with a previous union name that he still wears today. He even suggested that locals so inclined could indicate "formerly known as the International Brotherhood of Teamsters" on their stationery (p. 362). Another delegate, Ann McNeeley of Local 2000 in Bloomington, Minnesota, suggested that the name change could take place formally when the letterhead ran out.

However, what seemed to make the debate moot was how women themselves spoke up to resist a name change. In an interview after the conference, Cheryl Johnson, president of the ITWC, declared that the ITWC's stance was that the name change was not significant, revealing a liberal feminist perspective that resisted radical feminist dissent. Delegate Pat Kirkman of Local 696 in Topeka, Kansas, stated,

> As a woman I feel used when I am dragged into an issue against my will for the exploitation of women. This issue of changing the name has nothing to do with women and nothing to do with unity. This change is simply and sadly a political one. (IBT, 1996, p. 356)

Political division outweighed any potential efforts to promote gender equality. This rhetorical resistance to the norms of masculine rhetoric in the union proved to be ineffective because of the harsh backlash by female members. Kirkman went on to suggest that those promoting the name change were using women

> to make a savior when none is needed or requested. We will not be treated any differently, good or bad, regardless of what we call our union. If someone thinks women are second classed or not as much a Teamster, changing the name will not change any of these perceptions. In fact, all this silly sniveling will probably create more negative than positive. No one heard of a complaint about our name until the IBT raised it. And now women are forced to feel that they must fight for something they never lost. (p. 356)

Delegate Mary Jane Griffin of Local 710 in Chicago claimed that she was always respected but that this debate was being turned into a "sexist issue"; instead, she felt, "The Brotherhood of Teamsters means my family, my brothers and sisters" (p. 372).

The issue finally came down to those with moderate positions articulating their perspective. Delegate Kathy Peters of Local 31 in Delta, British Columbia, proved to offer an effective refutation of the name change by indicating that she herself was a feminist but still did not see the necessity in the change. After thanking "Brother Hoffa" for "freeing his supporters to vote their conscience on the proposed amendment," she stated,

> I struggled with [the name change decision] mightily before I rose today to speak in opposition. The debate took place between my heart, my feminist heart, and my mind. My heart argued that statistics have shown that girls and young women are influenced by gender-biased labels and titles. My head, on the other hand, reminded me that being a member of a brotherhood has never prevented me from achieving every goal I have set for myself in the 20 years I have been a Teamster. (p. 363)

Peters creates a dualism between women's needs as emotional—even though she calls on statistics as evidence—and the logic of men's recognition of the organization as a brotherhood. The outcome of the debate was a defeat of the proposal by a vote of 682 in favor and 1,127 against the name change. This result suggests that despite gender, many members are reluctant to let go of the narrative identification of the Teamsters as a brotherhood, perhaps because it might eliminate the emphasis on unity or cause men, the majority of original rank and file members, to feel less grounded in the Teamsters historical narrative. The importance of acknowledging the union as a brotherhood was articulated in 1971 when union employee James M. Barker wrote,

> The name of this union is the International Brotherhood of Teamsters. Mr. Hoffa and the men such as Frank Fitzsimmons,...and others formed a bond of friendship and brotherhood that lasted and inspired them all over the years, with J.R. Hoffa the driving force and brains. But the fact is they trusted each other in their common cause. Thus they made the union function good and made life better for all. As it finally turned out, even the employers admit that fact now. (p. 9)

Thus, through the exchange of opposing narrative perspectives, the union democratically negotiated to emphasize unity through the term brotherhood, and instead, to allow its internal (rather than external) rhetoric to offer space for competing notions of whom a member of the brotherhood could be. Consequently, rhetorical compliance and public narrative consistency was achieved through this debate; Teamsters women are implicitly acknowledged as sisters within the brotherhood through the continued use of the IBT title and are explicitly acknowledged as "sisters" in everyday union business.

Thus, narrative contention existed, and narrative literacy empowered organizational members to confront it. By deliberating what the term brotherhood meant to various members of various standpoints, the IBT narrative was reinterpreted; this could only happen through an active process of receiving and responding to various perspectives of those involved in competing narrative factions of the organization. Reviving the tenet of brotherhood within the union has served to unify those across generations of workers and of different genders who have variable ideas of what it means to be in a union and of what it means to be a Teamster "brother" or "sister" through a common, yet textured and flexible narrative. The IBT's history as a union that is ideologically conservative, yet militant in its organizing efforts, is also reflected rhetorically through the term brotherhood; however, the turbulent history of male domination has been revised to include women through an organizing principle that fuses the tensions of competing histories and meanings of Teamster unity.

Narrative literacy intersects the virtue of acknowledging multiple narrative perspectives with a view of literacy as socially constructed so that we can engage in awareness about how to participate in dialogue within and across contentious narrative perspectives. Through narrative literacy, Arnett's (2002) call for textured interpretation is met: we add the learning of new skills to our existing understanding of class structure and standpoint. Moving toward an understanding of narrative literacy promotes awareness of one's place in the world, the other's place in the world, and the unity of the contexts of both. Hopefully a focus on narrative literacy will help humans become more literate participants in dialogue among multiple, not just select, narratives.

Arnett (2002) says Freire implies that we can revolutionize our society if we can read others in a textured way. Therefore, today a person who is considered "literate" might be one who is able to adapt to new understandings of multiple narratives or conflicting perspectives on shared narratives. This type of literacy enables participation in the inevitable tensions and required ethics of dialogic exchange in postmodernity. Without this view of literacy, we are lost in our own worlds or, worse yet, locked rigidly into thinking we know others' narratives without first taking time to *learn* about them.

Narrative Literacy as Pragmatic and Ethical

Narrative literacy is a way to read others and their place in the world as we deliberate narrative meaning. Reflecting on a communication concept that is comparable to "reading" offers rich opportunities for reflection. Consider that all too often we learn that "skimming" too lightly can lead to missteps in meaning-making or serious confusion when a key point or important insight is missed; yet, we employ various reading strategies to survive and can become good at these if disciplined. Therefore, we can learn what to take in more deeply and what to let go of when developing narrative literacy. Some of what we "read" will filter into a revised understanding of a person and that person's communication; some will float away as less useful fragments of reality, as evident through the 1996 IBT convention minutes and how much is preserved yet little has carried on into the current organizational narratives. In either case, our communication and our narratives can then be modified as needed.

This process of narrative literacy was evident in the name change debate the IBT experienced in 1996; today, the union remains a brotherhood even as it strives to organize more and more women. Thus, while the brotherhood narrative continues to exist, it has been modified and enriched through the dialogue organizational members had in 1996; thus, these members increased their narrative literacy. Within the IBT, staying open to changes in interpretation within the organizational narrative was important to deliberating the organization's identification as a brotherhood. The bond of narrative in this case reflects a changing rather than fixed organizational ethos.

Acknowledging that narrative literacy requires reading the values and politics of the moral constructs or narratives of others, narrative literacy can be distinguished from standpoint theory. Julia T. Wood's (1992) understanding of standpoint theory acknowledges how "different social groups...develop particular skills, attitudes, ways of thinking, and understandings of life as a result of their standpoint in society" (p. 55). Since people are positioned in very different places in social hierarchies, those who are marginalized offer a perspective that is "less distorted, less biased, and more layers than those who occupy a more central standpoint" (Wood, 1992, p. 55). On the other hand, narrative literacy can enable us to understand the dialectic of standpoint and narrative; thus, we are uniquely positioned to gain more or less understanding of others' narratives based on our standpoint. A theoretical distinction would be that narrative literacy might enable us to learn about other narratives and standpoints whether we are standing in marginalized or central positions without suggesting that one of those positions is more capable of understanding. Many standpoints might be acknowledged during the deliberation of a narrative, yet until that deliberation occurs it might be unclear whose perspectives will be favored. The IBT convention minutes reveal the texture of organizational narratives through the many standpoint perspectives of those engaged in that debate.

Final Considerations for the Classroom

Discussing narrative literacy within the classroom can help us consider the twofold view of narrative, persuasion, and aesthetics that Fisher proposed. This might be useful to deliberating how we ethically invite, receive, or reject others within narrative contexts. As was evident in the IBT, communicative reading or narrative literacy, requires thought and heart, yet that does not mean we accept everything we "read." Reflecting on narrative literacy might also help us determine ways of entering into organizational narratives, even those within a classroom setting, as outsiders. For example, students from conservative backgrounds who don't understand the apparent contradiction of a liberal student who supports the right to bear arms could better understand that perspective if they stayed open to "reading others' narratives" rather than relying on assumptions or stereotypes about differences in values. Or, those who might want to use the Bible as persuasive evidence might be able to bolster their arguments by recognizing humbly that not everyone relies on that same moral construct or religious narrative as they do. Students might be helped to recognize that regardless of whether we believe someone's narrative is moral, we must acknowledge its existence. Students, like union members, must learn to negotiate multiple, competing, and sometimes contentious narratives by learning about them and positioning them as community-organizing moral constructs that we cannot ignore or wish away. Instead, narrative literacy obliges us to invite the ongoing conversation of life so we can decide what we will accept, respect, or let go.

Notes

1   The plural on "narratives" recognizes that we all engage in personal communicative narratives as well as multiple other narratives, including organizational narratives, the focus of this chapter.

2   Ruminski, E. (2003). "A New Kind of Literacy."

3   This paper was presented at a Duquesne University Department of Communication and Rhetorical Studies graduate student colloquium in 2002.

4   I coined this metaphor during discussion following Roberts' and Moroco's colloquium presentation, developed the metaphor in a course paper with Dr. Ronald Arnett and then expand the metaphor theoretically in conference presentations: Ruminski, E. (2003) "The Metaphor of Narrative Literacy" and Ruminski, E. (2003b) "A New Kind of Literacy."

5   Although McCown did not note this, adelfos in Greek means brother and filia means friendship, so to call Philadelphia the city of "sisterly love" would be etymologically incorrect.

References

Agonito, R. (1977). *The history of ideas on woman: A source book.* New York: Perigee.

Aristotle. (2004). *Rhetoric.* (W. R. Roberts, Trans.). New York: Dover.

Arnett, R. C. (2001). Dialogic civility as pragmatic ethical praxis: An interpersonal metaphor for the public domain. *Communication Theory, 11,* 315-338.

———. (2002). Paulo Freire's revolutionary pedagogy: From a story-centered communication ethics to a narrative-centered communication ethics. *Qualitative Inquiry, 8,* 489-510.

Arnett, R. C. & Arneson, P. (1999). *Dialogic civility in a cynical age: Community, hope, and interpersonal relationships.* Albany: State University of New York Press.

Christ, W. G., & Potter, J. (2002). Media literacy, media education, and the academy. *Journal of Communication.* 48, 5-15.

Donovan, J. (2000). *Feminist theory: The intellectual traditions.* 3rd ed. New York: Continuum.

Fisher, W. R. (2000). Narration as a human communication paradigm: The case of public moral argument. In Carl R. Burgchardt (Ed.), *Readings in rhetorical criticism* (pp. 290-312). State College, PA: Strata.

Freire, P. (2002). *Pedagogy of the oppressed.* New York: Continuum.

Freire, P. & Macedo, D. (1987). *Literacy: Reading the word and the world.* Westport, CT: Bergin & Garvey.

Gadamer, H.G. (1976). *Philosophical hermeneutics.* Berkeley: University of California Press.

Hirsch, Jr., E.D., Kett, J. F., & Trefil, J. (2002). *The new dictionary of cultural literacy.* Boston: Houghton Mifflin.

International Brotherhood of Teamsters (IBT). (1996). 25th International Convention Proceedings. July 15-19. Philadelphia, PA.

————. (2000). Strategic Planning Committee. Two Million in 2000. Interim Report. Miami: IBT.

Leiter, R. D. (1974). *The teamsters union: A study of its economic impact.* New York: Octagon.

Moroco, L. & Roberts, K. (2002). Narrative fluency and vernacular discourse: The case of black English. Unpublished Manuscript.

Ratzinger, Cardinal J. (1996). *The meaning of Christian brotherhood.* San Francisco, CA: Ignatius.

Ruminski, E. (2003). "The metaphor of narrative literacy: An initial exploration." National Communication Association convention, Miami, Florida.

————. (2003b). "A new kind of literacy: Reading postmodern narratives." Pennsylvania Communication Association conference, State College, Pennsylvania.

Willis, A. I. (1997). Focus on research: Historical considerations. *Language Arts, 74,* 387-397.

Wood, J. T. (1992). Gender and moral voice: Moving from women's nature to standpoint epistemology. *Women's Studies in Communication, 15,* 1-24.

Chapter 7

Dialogue as the Labor of Care: The Necessity of a Unity of Contraries within Interpersonal Communication

Marie Baker Ohler

For there are many great deeds done in the small struggles of life. There is a determined though unseen bravery, which defends itself foot to foot in the darkness against the fatal invasions of necessity and of baseness. Noble and mysterious triumphs which no eye sees, which no renown rewards, which no flourish of triumph salutes. Life, misfortunes, isolation, abandonment, poverty, are battlefields which have their heroes; obscure heroes, sometimes greater than the illustrious heroes.

Strong and rare natures are thus created; misery, almost always a stepmother, is sometimes a mother; privation gives birth to power of soul and mind; distress is the nurse of self-respect; misfortune is a good breast for great souls.

—(Hugo, Les Miserables, p. 588)

"Dialogue as the labor of care," a suggested communicative ethic for this historical moment, unfolds a vision of how the philosophy of dialogue can assist us as human beings to enact care in our daily lives. In the end, caring is a unity of contraries: blessing and burden, joy and suffering, necessity and triumph. The invitation of dialogue into the communicative life of caring requires courage and thus creates strong and rare natures.

The impetus of this vision comes from the work of Martin Buber, whose ideas have changed the way we view communication and enrich the way we view caring (Baxter & Cissna, 2003). The additional metaphor of labor, provided by the work of Hannah Arendt (1958), allows for a deeper understanding of caring. Buber and Arendt, both Jewish philosophers working from their World War II perspective, provide an especially textured understanding of the pain and suffering of the concept of care. The metaphor of labor reveals and emphasizes that care is not only a necessity for human communicative life, but is at the same time a blessing and a burden. The necessity of labor opens the conversation, through the notion of care as an imperative for everyday communicative life. Joy and suffering, blessing and burden, necessity and triumph emphasize the fact that life is best lived in the unity of contraries.

A communicative ethic such as dialogue as the labor of care is called for because of the current postmodern historical moment that is marked by the loss of narrative background, routine cynicism, extreme individualism, and existential mistrust between persons. Furthermore, the ongoing devaluation of caring exacerbates the problem within interpersonal communication. The communicative problem of this moment has come to the foreground because in recent years many people, for many different reasons, find themselves in caring relationships, and they are at a loss as to how to communicatively enact the caring needed.

Introduction

The communicative relationship between dialogue and care has been implicitly assumed and on occasion made explicit as a suggestion by authors such as Richard Johannesen (2000) and Nel Noddings (1984). Through Martin Buber's theory of dialogue and foundational literature related to care, this work points to the necessity of a more textured understanding of the connection between dialogue and care. The purpose of this chapter is to make explicit this relationship. Through Hannah Arendt's concept of labor, dialogue and care are united in a metaphor that frames care as a unity of contraries, blessing and burden, joy and suffering. The nature of caring is both obligatory and relational—caring is an action that yields life-related communicative outcomes in the context of everyday public and private human interaction.

In his novel *Les Miserables*, Victor Hugo (1961) asserted that many great deeds occur in the small struggles of our everyday toil. Caring is one of those deeds. Through the creation of the communication ethic dialogue as the labor of care, one finds Hugo's comment on "illustrious heroes" even more profound. In this passage one sees the metaphor, dialogue as the labor of care, unfold. Through the invitation of dialogue into the communicative life of caring, souls on the battlefields of life find bravery, triumphs, and rewards that allow them to continue to face the invasions of necessity. *Les Miserables* exemplifies the idea that life is not lived in a singular fashion; in fact, life is best lived in the unity of contraries. In the case of caring, the unity of contraries, joy and suffering, blessing and burden, necessity and triumph allow the full impact of a meaningful human existence.

The relationship of dialogue and care is examined in the following pages through the dialogic philosophy of Martin Buber and the nature of care as constituted in human communication. The unity of dialogue and care is given greater depth and understanding through Hannah Arendt's imperative of labor. The metaphor driving this essay-dialogue as the labor of care–is the culmination of these perspectives into a communicative philosophy of care that reengages care as a value central to both public and private life.

Buber and Arendt

The call of this historical moment, to reengage care, is made explicit through the unification of Buberian dialogue and care vis-à-vis Arendt's labor imperative. From the work of Martin Buber comes the theory of dialogue that compels an understanding of human communication situated in relation (Anderson, Cissna & Arnett, 1994). This is significant because Buber embeds dialogue within the "lived concrete, the everyday reality" of human existence (Friedman, 1960, p. v). Buber's (1963) philosophy is a philosophy of the "interhuman," life lived in relation (p. 83). Buber offered ideas that are always situated within, and responsive to, the historical moment. Furthermore, Buber's philosophical anthropology has been hailed as significant to the field of interpersonal communication. According to Ronald C. Arnett (2005), "emphasizing philosophical anthropology situates Buber's dialogic project and privileges a space for the discipline of communication" (p. 77).

To bring the metaphor of dialogue as the labor of care to fruition, this chapter also employs the theory of the human condition articulated by Hannah Arendt, who writes from a political theorist's perspective and focuses the majority of her thinking on life–the human condition (Kristeva, 2001). As such, the focus here is primarily on Arendt's writing in *The Human Condition* in which she made known the intimate relationship between labor and action in human life. This relationship implies care as central to all human relations. Like Buber, Arendt's ideas are concerned with responding to specific happenings in a historical moment—to specific experiences in people's lives. Arendt's contribution to this discussion lies in her ability to connect philosophical thought to everyday life–a valuable perspective when coupled with the textured view of dialogue presented by Buber.

Dialogue, labor, and care are metaphors that involve the "mud" of everyday life (Arnett & Arneson, 1999) and come together to offer hope for walking through this "mud" as people living in relation to others. When joined together, these metaphors frame a communicative ethic—"a picture of a world that we can try to invite" (Arnett, 1986, p. 2). This communicative ethic is dialogue as the labor of care.

The Call of Care

The call of responsibility to care has been a call heard throughout time. Care has always been relegated to the private sphere and continually devalued. However, this particular historical moment calls us to reexamine not only the importance of care but also the necessity of care to our daily communicative lives.

Owing to the changing face of the family and the changing circumstances that demand people to reengage caring, people are finding themselves in the position of caring, communicatively unequipped. Living in a postmodern moment, where existential mistrust, routine cynicism, and an extreme focus on the self are pervasive, the communicative life of caring finds itself in crisis. For these reasons, dialogue as the labor of care is especially relevant to this particular historical moment. Martin Buber argued that if we invite dialogue into our daily lives we can overcome the massive mistrust that pervades our communicative life. Dialogue as the labor of care calls for a reengagement of care as a value central to human relations. The communicative importance of care is realized through the connection of dialogue to care.

Buber's theory of dialogue is the foundation of this work because dialogue is intimately connected to care. Arendt's (1958) ideas concerning labor emphasize the necessity of dialogue in the communicative life of caring that has both a blessing and a burden. Moreover, Arendt's ideas regarding action illuminate the fact that caring occurs in webs of human relationships and stresses the imperative of differentiation within the communicative life of caring for others. Through the touchstones of care—obligation, relation, and significant outcomes–the work of Buber and Arendt frame a deeper examination of the connection between dialogue and caring. Here, the intertexture of the suggested metaphor dialogue as the labor of care is made explicit, enhancing understanding and making its application and engagement possible in everyday life.

To make this intertextuality sound, the central use of Buber's theory of dialogue is coupled here with the imperative of labor as necessity found in Arendt. The metaphor of labor as necessity moves the idea of dialogue out of an advocacy of consumption and into productivity. The connection between dialogue and care takes on more significance to interpersonal communicative life with the addition of Arendt to the conversation, because Arendt's conception of labor within the private sphere points to the desire to escape from care and the obligations of "life," a sentiment echoed in the devaluation of care today. What Arendt's theories bring to the conversation is an imperative–care as an inescapable communicative action that is a blessing and a burden.

The following section explores Buber's dialogic theory and Arendt's conceptions of labor and action and their undeniable connection to caring by looking at how these ideas correlate to the metaphors established through the care literature. The work begins with the care metaphor of obligation and moves through the second and third metaphors of relation and significant outcomes, developing each in terms of Buber's conception of dialogue and Arendt's understanding of the human condition.

Obligation: A Binding Promise to the Other

As human beings, we have an obligation to labor that is necessary for our continued existence. As human beings living in the world with others, we have an obligation to care for one another not only for our survival, but also for the realization of becoming truly human. Obligation is defined as "[s]omething by which a person is bound or obliged to do certain things and which arises out of a sense of duty or results from custom, law, etc.; a binding promise, contract, sense of duty, etc; indebtedness; a debt of gratitude"(Wolf, 1974, p. 1336). The metaphors of responsibility, guilt, and labor are the significant metaphors that emerge in one's engagement with an obligation. From the call of responsibility one finds himself/herself bound to the other through a sense of promise and/or duty. When one fails to accept the call, guilt is the mechanism that calls one back to responsibility. As an obligation, a binding promise or duty, the action of caring requires labor on the part of the one caring and the one cared for.

Dialogue as the labor of care is rooted in the essential ideas found within the philosophical writings of Buber and Arendt. The first idea, and one of the most foundational, is obligation. Dialogue and care both require that one recognize his/her obligation to the other, to themselves, and to the world. In both dialogue and care there is a call to responsibility that requires a recognition of and engagement in the labor necessary on the part of those involved. Through the necessity of labor one finds joy and suffering, blessing and burden.

Obligation is fundamental to the current conception of caring. Scholars such as Mayeroff (1972), Gaylin (1976), Gilligan (1982), Noddings (1984), and Tronto (1993) all incorporate obligation within their explanation of caring. According to these "care" scholars, caring begins as an obligation to the other. Communicatively constituted, responsibility requires response, response of the one caring to the needs of the other and response by the one being cared for to acknowledge that the caring is received. The caring relationship calls one into responsibility and holds him/her accountable to their obligation to the other. Obligation presupposes responsibility for the other.

The work of Buber and Arendt are likewise philosophically rooted in obligation. The richness of a connection between dialogue and care opens up through Buber's understanding of responsibility and guilt, and through Arendt's conception of labor. For Buber, responsibility is *response*; response to a call from the other; and for Arendt, labor is the necessity of answering the call of the other. A more developed look into each of these metaphors as pointing to the need for a unified understanding of dialogue and labor in relation to a communicative ethic of care is necessary.

Responsibility: The Response to the Other

Martin Buber's (1970) philosophical anthropology begins with the presupposition that life is lived in relation. Authentic existence can only occur through the invitation of dialogue into relationship. Responsibility and guilt are essential metaphors in the life of dialogue and caring relationships. Buber (1963) indicated three important elements of responsibility: first, the one that is called into responsibility, second, the situation itself, and third, the one who addresses the other and calls him/her into responsibility.

Buber explicitly described the role of those called into responsibility. According to Buber (1963), the one called must respond to fulfill his/her obligation to the other, to the world, and to himself. His/her response depends primarily on his/her attentiveness and whether or not he/she responds with his/her whole being.

For Buber (1955), responsibility means response, response on the part of the one called by the concrete moment. It is the obligation, or in other words, responsibility, of each particular person called to respond. Buber stressed that responsibility as response means that one is attentive to a concrete situation and responds in a unique and authentic way. According to Buber, there are concrete hours that address one, but each person must first see the signs of address, hear what calls, and feel the address of the other. Seeing, hearing, and feeling are the ways in which one can be attentive to the moment. When one is attentive, they are then able to understand and respond. It is response for Buber that brings authentic life into existence. When there is address and response, Buber (1955) states, there is life. Our responsibility to the other, to the world, to the moment, to ourselves comes in the actual responding. Each concrete moment speaks; it is the person who responds to the call of the situation who is attentive.

The person who is attentive has an obligation in each situation that calls his/her presence into responsibility. For Buber, this can only happen when the one called into responsibility responds with his/her whole being in a unique way. Responding with one's whole being implies that one enters the situation and acts with the whole of one's substance. "Responsibility, to Buber, means hearing the unreduced claim of each hour in its crudeness and disharmony and answering for it out of the depths of one's being" (Friedman, 1983, p. 123). The one called into responsibility is called to respond. They can rise to that occasion by being attentive and honestly taking part in the life of another. Real response requires a unique, authentic response of the whole being. When responding, the one called not only responds to the other, but they also respond to the particular hour, the unique situation.

Buber not only wrote about the role of the one being called into responsibility, but, he also emphasizes the importance of the situation. Buber (1955) argues, "Every living situation has, like a new-born child, a new face, that has never been seen before and will never come again. It demands of you a reaction which cannot be prepared beforehand. It demands nothing of what is past. It demands presence, responsibility, it demands you" (p. 114). Here Buber's words remind us that each situation, each moment, each person is unlike any other and cannot be answered with a formula or a technique. Response to the situation, as Buber might say, is equally important as a response to the person when one is called into responsibility. Each situation is new and demands a unique answer, despite any similarity the situation has to those of the past. It is the responsibility of the attentive person to recognize the uniqueness of the situation and answer for it.

Responsibility is response—response by someone, the one called, response to a unique situation, the concrete moment, and response to someone. The final element of Buber's conception of responsibility is responsibility to someone. Responsibility involves the one called taking an active part in the life of the other. Dialogue requires one to turn toward another and respond; response requires one to take part in their lives.

The other is the one who makes the address, reaches out, the one to whom there must be a response. The other in his/her particular situation makes a claim in responsibility. Buber (1955) believed that one is answerable to the other. In the address or the call of the other, there is a claim put on the one for whom it is intended. There is an obligation on the part of the one called to respond. In making this call, there is a leap of faith by the other that the one called will hear the call and respond. This leap of faith implies trust on the part of the one calling. The one making the claim offers the other a sacred trust, the response of the one called determines the continuation or dissolution of that trust.

Obligation and responsibility require the one called to answer; when that person fails to respond, Buber (1955) said that trust is lost, responsibility becomes a "phantom," and life's character of mutuality is dissipated (p. 45). When one fails to respond, genuine meeting cannot occur. For there to ever be a possibility for dialogue to exist, something must call persons back into relation. Both obligation and responsibility are enacted in relation. We are called, ever reminded of our obligation and responsibility by authentic guilt.

Guilt: The Savoir of Trust

Buber described responsibility as response. Within responsibility, Buber emphasized the one called is obligated to the moment and to the other. The one is called to respond. Response on behalf of the one called asks him/her to be attentive and respond with his/her whole being. Response means answering not only the particular other but also the concrete moment. Response, for Buber, is necessary to build trust between persons and invite dialogue into life. Response is necessary for human beings to build a world worth living in. But, as Buber pointed out, people ignore the call to responsibility every day. When this happens, trust is lost and the opportunity for dialogue dies. However, according to Buber (1963) all is not lost. Sometimes even when someone ignores a call to responsibility, the moment seizes the one who ignored his/her responsibility and he/she is called back to responsibility through guilt. When the one called returns, responsibility can be reborn.

Guilt is the human condition that gives rebirth to trust, to responsibility, to man. Guilt, for Buber, is existentially tied to responsibility. For it is in failing to respond to a legitimate claim that we are guilty. Like responsibility, Buber described three important and similar elements of guilt. However, before exploring these elements, this section first clarifies Buber's conception of existential guilt. Once clarified, this section looks at Buber's emphasis on the elements of guilt. Similar to his description of responsibility wherein one sees the importance of the one called, the situation, and the one calling the other into responsibility, in describing guilt Buber emphasized the locus of guilt, the one who is guilty, and finally the other to whom one is guilty.

True guilt, which Buber (1963) distinguished from neurotic guilt, is existential guilt and has to do with one's engagement with the world. Existential guilt is ignited when one fails in how he/she relates to other people. Existential guilt is dialogic. Through guilt one recognizes their failure to respond, their failure to themselves, and their failure to the other. The existence of responsibility requires and demands the existence of guilt. For it is guilt that brings one back to responsibility when they fail to respond or when they respond inadequately. Existential guilt is what ties human beings to the world and to each other. Existential guilt reminds one of his/her responsibility to the other.

Just as one is responsible to the other, to the moment, to the world, to God, to themselves, when one fails to respond he/she is guilty toward the other, the world, the moment, God, and themselves. This is crucial in understanding Buber's conception of guilt and its relationship to responsibility. Guilt is the condition that reminds one that he/she is related to something other than themselves (Friedman, 1960, p. 104). Therefore, according to Buber (1963), guilt is not located in the guilty party. Guilt is not located in the other. Guilt, for Buber, is located in the bond between them. "One is not answerable for it [guilt] either to oneself alone or to society apart from oneself, but to that very bond between oneself and others through which one again and again discovers the direction in which one can authenticate one's existence" (Friedman, 1965, p. 48). When one fails to respond, when one fails in his/her responsibility, it is guilt that brings him/her back and points him/her in the direction of responsibility. It is guilt that points him/her back to relation, back to the other, back to authentic existence.

Guilt is the element that pushes one to seek atonement. It is in seeking atonement that responsibility, trust, and authentic existence can be reborn. Authentic existence can only be found in turning toward the other in relation; therefore, guilt is inextricably tied to relations with others. Through the invocation of guilt, persons recognize their responsibility and seek to set their relationships right (Friedman, 1965). Through the self-illumination of guilt, the guilty party realizes that it has failed to respond and thus seeks reconciliation from the other. Through guilt, the guilty person recognizes his/her responsibility to other and seeks atonement. Reconciliation turns the guilty party back toward the other seeking to help him/her as far as possible. At times, Buber argued that it is impossible to make reparations to the one for whom one has failed to respond. But reconciliation can still be found in responding to the next address.

Obligation, from Buber's perspective, finds richness and texture in the metaphors of responsibility and guilt. Life lived in relation becomes fulfilled in response to the address of the other. Buber's dialogic theory asserts that responsibility is response. Each person is responsible for the moment, responsible to the other who addresses them. In answering/responding to the address, relation comes alive.

In attempting to answer, one's whole being is required. Responsibility calls one to be attentive and to respond in a unique manner. It is also one's responsibility to recognize that each address is unique. Therefore, it requires a unique response. Responsibility requires one to take part in another's life. This other is the one who calls one into responsibility. In reaching out the other is offering trust and demanding loyalty. It is one's response that dictates how the relationship proceeds. If one fails to respond or responds inadequately and recognizes this failure, he/she is thrown into the condition of existential guilt.

Guilt is essential to the life of responsibility and relationships. Guilt is found not in the one called or the one calling but in the bond between them. This bond is what initiates guilt, points one toward the other, encourages one to seek reconciliation, and eventually has the power to restore the relationship. It is through guilt that one recognizes one's failure and encourages one to attempt to make reparations. It is in seeking reconciliation that trust, relation, and dialogue can be reborn. Buber (1955) emphasized the connection of responsibility to life: "I know no fullness but each mortal hour's fullness of claim and responsibility. Though far from being equal to it, yet I know that in the claim I am claimed and may respond in responsibility, and know who speaks and demands a response" (p. 14). This passage reveals the essence of obligation as Buber envisioned it. This guilt pulls one back into relationship through the central coordinates of obligation and responsibility. Arendt outlined the way in which these coordinates, responsibility and guilt, are enacted in labor between persons.

Distinguishing the Metaphors

The work of Hannah Arendt is imperative to the connection between dialogue and caring because of Arendt's (1958) distinctions between and ideas concerning the public and private spheres, and labor and action. Before inviting Arendt's work into the intertexture of dialogue, labor, and care, it will be helpful to distinguish between and briefly explain her conception of public, private, and social and labor, work, and action.

Arendt (1958) drew distinct lines between the public and private spheres of human existence, arguing that these realms have been distinct entities since at least the rise of the city-state. According to Arendt, the private sphere is the realm of the household and the family. The purpose of the private sphere is the maintenance of life itself. According to Arendt, "the distinctive trait of the household was that in it men lived together because they were driven by their wants and needs" (p. 30). Necessity is the driving force behind all activities in the private realm.

The public sphere, on the other hand, was, for Arendt, the political realm. Freedom and equality are found in the public sphere. One is able to enter the public realm, when one has mastered the necessities of the private realm. The public realm is the place where "men" come together to be seen and heard and achieve not only freedom and equality, they are able to achieve individuality. In the public realm "men could show who they really and inexchangeably were" (Arendt, 1958, p. 41).

The blurring of public and private spheres of existence has, Arendt (1958) argued, given rise to the "social" realm of existence. The lines are blurred because "we see the body of peoples and political communities in the image of a family whose everyday affairs have to be taken care of by a gigantic, nation-wide administration of housekeeping" (p. 28). Arendt described the social sphere as one that is neither public nor private but it destroys both the public and the private. The social realm, for Arendt, denies people of both a place in the home and in the world. According to Arendt, the most dangerous aspect of the social is that one loses one's uniqueness. To be accepted into the social realm, one must conform to the opinions and interests of the social. In the social sphere, there is no differentiation.

It is of vital importance to recognize the danger of Arendt's conception of the social, a demand for conformity, and an absence of uniqueness. As caring can occur in both the public and private realms and as this chapter employs Arendt's metaphors of labor and action, there is the dangerous possibility of blurring the lines between public and private. In recognizing the differences we go forward carefully explaining how the engagement of care involves both action and labor in both the public and private spheres of human interaction.

In the distinction between public, private, and social, the additional metaphors of labor, work, and action emerge. Arendt (1958) distinguished between the activities fundamental to the public and private spheres and the human condition: labor, work, and action. Labor, the necessary activity that corresponds to the biological life cycle, assures not only the life of the individual, but also the species. Labor is an activity engaged in the private sphere. The following section describes Arendt's conception of labor.

Arendt's Notion of Labor

Work is the activity directed toward the production of durable human artifacts for use and enjoyment. "Work provides an 'artificial' world of things, distinctly different from all natural surroundings...The human condition of work is worldliness" (p. 7). In the activity of work, one makes something, that is, a table that has the possibility to remain in the world long after its creator is gone. Work produces something tangible. The metaphor of work is not employed in the metaphorical web of this chapter.

Action is the third and final activity Arendt (1958) described as given to the human condition. "Action, the only activity that goes on directly between men without the intermediary of things or matter, corresponds to human condition of plurality" (p. 7). Action occurs in the public realm in the company of equals. Those in the public realm are equal because they are all human beings and because they are participating in the public realm, uniquely. Action is employed here in connection to the care metaphor of relation. The use of labor and action as driving metaphors behind the connection between dialogue and care is crucial, as the following connects Arendt's imperative of labor to the care metaphor of obligation and Buber's metaphors of responsibility and guilt.

Labor: The Necessity of Life That Bears Blessing and Burden

Buber's ideas of responsibility and guilt are encompassed in the work of Hannah Arendt through her concept of labor. Like responsibility and guilt, labor is integrally tied to the obligatory call of the other. Arendt's conception of labor reminds us that obligation binds one to a duty, and that these duties are part of the necessity of life. As a necessary part of everyday living, labor illuminates the truth of life: our responsibility to the other is both a blessing and a burden. This unity of contraries configures how we live and interact. It is the foundation of who we are as individuals and as a community. Labor is the call of the other on each person—an imperative to act out of responsibility in the interest of someone other than oneself.

Labor as Futile: The Unending Burden

In describing the human condition Hannah Arendt (1958) defined labor as "the activity which corresponds to the biological process of the human body, whose spontaneous growth, metabolism, and eventual decay are bound to the vital necessities, produced and fed into the life process by labor. The human condition of labor is life itself" (p. 7). Through this initial definition and Arendt's expanded explanation, it becomes obvious that although labor is a necessary part of human existence, it is the exhausting activity of the human condition that most people try to escape.

As mentioned previously, labor is the activity bound to the private sphere. Arendt (1958) argued that labor is repetitive (with no beginning and no end); labor leaves no trace, nothing worthy of remembrance; and labor is the activity in which there is no distinction between persons. For these reasons, Arendt said that labor is a burden that man views as futile. According to Arendt (1958), "Life becomes a burden to man because of his innate repugnance to futility (pointlessness). This burden is all the heavier because labor is urgent and actually forced upon man by necessity, as the elementary need of life" (pp. 118-119).

Arendt's conception of labor begins with the fact that labor is part of the unending life cycle to which one is bound and cannot escape. As labor is a necessity and part of the unending life cycle, labor has no beginning and no end. Labor, for Arendt, is unending for both individuals and the human race. For Arendt, "the laboring activity never comes to an end as long as life lasts; it is endlessly repetitive" (Baehr, 2000, p. 171). As part of the unending life process, Arendt explained the circular nature of labor. Labor is a cyclical movement with no beginning and no end. The cyclical, unending nature of labor is one of the first reasons persons view labor as futile.

As part of the unending necessity of human existence, labor is endlessly repetitive and, according to Arendt (1958), never produces anything but life itself. "It is indeed the mark of all laboring that it leaves nothing behind, that the result of its effort is almost as quickly consumed as the effort is spent. And yet this effort, despite its futility, is born of a great urgency and motivated by a more powerful drive than anything else, because life itself depends on it" (p. 87). Labor leaves no trace, no monument, and no great work worthy of remembrance. Again, labor never produces anything but life itself. This is the second reason persons view labor as futile.

As labor is bound to the necessities of life, it is subject to the private sphere, in which, according to Arendt (1958), "man is neither together with the world nor with other people, but alone with his body, facing the naked necessity to keep himself alive" (p. 212). Subject to the private sphere and alone with oneself, labor makes persons incapable of distinction and, therefore, incapable of action and speech. The inability of distinction is the third and final reason persons view labor as futile.

Labor, bound to the private sphere, makes distinction between persons impossible. Human beings, since at least the rise of the city-state, have continually tried to escape the necessity of labor. This chapter recognizes these conditions of labor as important contributors to the devaluation of activities such as care. However, through the intertexture of care, the imperative of labor, this chapter points to Arendt's more powerful argument regarding labor. Labor is, for Arendt, an inescapable necessity addressed in daily life through which human beings can engage the intensity of life. Through the necessity of labor, human beings can experience the unity of contraries—joy and suffering, blessing and burden that make life meaningful.

Labor as Necessity: The Inescapable Burden

As stated earlier Arendt (1958) suggested that "labor assures not only the life of the individual but the life of the species" (p. 8). Being a vital necessity to both individuals and the human race, labor can be seen as both an obligation and responsibility in the interpersonal communicative lives of people. Arendt's conception of labor–a vital necessity of life–viewed in the light of human relations binds the responsibility of inviting dialogue into communicative life. Arendt argued, "Labor, unlike all other human activities, stands under the sign of necessity, the necessity of subsisting" (Baehr, 2000, p. 171). As such, the obligation of labor is necessary for existence of oneself and of others.

As understood by Buber, this kind of investment is enacted through a call to responsibility that is part of everyone's existence. Each person is answerable to concrete moments that call him/her to respond. The imperative of labor is, then, the innate reminder of one to his/her obligation to respond to the other. The labor of the responding requires one to turn to the other with one's whole being and to respond to the particular situation. This labor—necessity—points to the communicative obligation at the core of human life. Pragmatically one needs to understand the unity of contraries burden and that essential meaningfulness rests within labor—to toil and to take something seriously.

Labor as the Unity of Contraries: Blessing and Burden

Labor as a necessity is an obligation born in the midst of contradiction. While necessary for life, it is hallmarked by the tension of blessing and burden, joy and suffering, labor itself and action. Arendt's conception of labor as part of human communicative life underscores the reality that we live in the midst of contradictions in search of unity and coherence. Life is shaped in the between of a unity of contraries.

Labor is, according to Arendt, part of the human condition. Life requires pain ("toil and trouble") and effort but in return gives back liveliness and vitality. Arendt believes that the "life of the gods"–a life without the experience wrought in the midst of contradictions– would not fulfill the life of human beings. Our condition as humans "is such that pain and effort are not just symptoms which can be removed without changing life itself; they are rather the modes in which life itself, together with the necessity to which it is bound, makes itself felt" (Arendt, 1958, p. 120). Labor, for Arendt, is the part of the human condition that allows life to be trusted—to know that life is real. Labor is the element that gives life its force and intensity, and though it is a burden, without its presence Arendt believed human beings would lose the vitality of life itself (p. 121).

For Arendt, this vitality of life as lived within the obligation of labor allows a person one of the only true forms of happiness, because one fulfills their responsibility to the necessity of life. Trusting life and knowing its "realness" is born out of labor. Happiness is living in this reality. As people respond to the imperative of labor, their rewards are received in "nature's fertility"—in one's confidence that they have done their part (Baehr, 2000, p. 172). Herein lies labor's unity of contraries. Labor is a burden of life, an obligation one cannot escape, and a blessing, a source of happiness in living out what is real and the blessing of life as a whole is inherent in labor:

> The blessing of labor is that effort and gratification follow each other as closely as producing and consuming, so that happiness is a concomitant of the process itself. There is no lasting happiness and contentment for human beings outside the prescribed cycle of painful exhaustion and pleasurable regeneration...An element of laboring is present in all human activities, even the highest as they are as "routine" jobs by which we make our living and keep ourselves alive. Their very repetitiveness, which more often than not we feel to be a burden that exhausts us, is what provides

that minimum of animal contentment for which the great and meaningful spells of joy that are rare and never last, can never be a substitute, and without which the longer lasting though equally rare spells of real grief and sorrow could hardly be borne. (Baehr, 2000, pp. 172-173)

Labor is a necessity of life that requires effort, toil and trouble, and painful exhaustion but at the same time gives back pleasurable regeneration, contentment, and joy. The meaningful happiness found in labor allows human beings to bear the grief and sorrow of life with full joy at the truth of what they have come to know.

Labor is a burden of life, an obligation one cannot escape, and a blessing, a source of happiness in living out what is real. The author recognizes Arendt's use of labor as necessity—a necessity to the interpersonal communicative lives of those involved in relationships. Labor is the necessary human activity that brings life's unity of contraries together.

Dialogue as the labor of care begins with the care metaphor of obligation. Obligation is seen as a binding promise made to the other, a duty in which one is obliged to do something for another. Through the metaphors of responsibility, guilt, and labor, obligation takes on a communicative nature. For Buber, responsibility means response. To fulfill one's responsibility to the other, one must respond with one's whole being in a unique and authentic fashion. Response requires the one called into responsibility to be attentive to the call of the other, the uniqueness of the other, and the uniqueness of the situation. Guilt calls one back to responsibility when one fails in their obligation, thus permitting the rebirth of trust and human relationships. Labor is human activity that emphasizes the necessity of obligation to human communicative lives. The labor of responding requires one to engage in the toil and trouble of obligation, thus permitting those involved to feel the full impact of human existence. Labor not only emphasizes necessity, but labor also permits one to engage in the unity of contraries that is life, joy and suffering, blessing and burden. There are many great deeds done in the small struggles of life. When one bravely invites dialogue into a caring relation with another and recognizes the communicative labor required, there is triumph.

References

Anderson, R., Cissna, K. N., & Arnett, R. C. (1994). *The reach of dialogue: Confirmation, voice, and community.* Cresskill, NJ: Hampton Press.

Arendt, H. (1958). *The human condition.* Chicago: University of Chicago Press.

Arnett, R. C. (1986). *Communication and community: Implications of Martin Buber's dialogue.* Carbondale: Southern Illinois University Press.

———. (2005). *Dialogic confession: Bonhoeffer's rhetoric of responsibility.* Carbondale: Southern Illinois University Press.

Arnett, R. C. & Arneson, P. (1999). *Dialogic civility in a cynical age: Community, hope and interpersonal relationships.* Albany: State University of New York Press.

Baehr, P. (Ed.). (2000). *The portable Hannah Arendt.* New York: Penguin Books.

Baxter, L. & Cissna, K. (2003). *Dialogue: Theorizing difference in communication studies.* New York: Sage.

Buber, M. (1955). *Between man and man.* (R. G. Smith, Trans.). Boston: Beacon Press.

———. (1963). *Pointing the way.* (M. Friedman, Trans.). New York: Harper & Row.

———. (1970). *I and thou.* (W. Kaufmann, Trans). New York: Touchstone.

Friedman, M. S. (1960). *Martin Buber: The life of dialogue.* New York: Harper & Brothers.

Friedman, M. (Ed.). (1965). Introductory essay. *The knowledge of man* (pp. 11-58). New York: Harper & Row.

———. (1983). *The confirmation of otherness in family, community, and society.* New York: Pilgrim Press.

Gaylin, W. (1976). *Caring.* New York: Random House.

Gilligan, C. (1982). *In a different voice: Psychological theory and women's development.* Cambridge, MA: Harvard University Press.

Hugo, V. (1961). *Les miserables.* New York: Fawcett Premier.

Johannesen, R. L. (2000). Nel Noddings's uses of Martin Buber's philosophy of dialogue. *The Southern Communication Journal, 65* (2-3, Winter), 151-100.

Kristeva, J. (2001). *Hannah Arendt.* (R. Guberman, Trans.). New York: Columbia University Press.

Mayeroff, M. (1972). *On caring.* New York: Harper Perennial.

Noddings, N. (1984). *Caring: A feminine approach to ethics & moral education.* Los Angeles: University of California Press.

Tronto, J. C. (1993). *Moral boundaries.* New York: Routledge.

Wolf, H. B. (1974). *Webster's new collegiate dictionary.* Springfield, MA: G & C Merriam.

Chapter 8

Engaging the Rhetorical Consciousness of an Organization for Dynamic Communicative Exchange

S. Alyssa Groom

In this chapter, the rhetorical consciousness of an organization—a praxis mode of organizational communicative interaction for the purposes of ethical engagement—is posited as a philosophical and practical point of departure for a communicative framework of an organization. Moving beyond the established necessity of integrated marketing communication for coherence and consistency throughout the organizational communication process, the intent of this work is to advance the idea of organizational communication as a storied phenomenon grounded in a commitment to the story of an organization before the integration of its messages across various mediums. The approach, therefore, is from the inside-out, focusing on Calvin O. Schrag's (1986) "communicative praxis"—communication about something, by someone, for someone—as a framework for explicating the rhetorical consciousness of an organization as well as for moving organizational communication into the realm of story-centered engagement.

Introduction

The value of organizational communication in establishing marketplace position as well as in building and maintaining customer relationships cannot be overstated. In a historical moment shaped by an accelerated rate of technological change, intracultural lifestyles, and a heightened commoditization of personal preference, the value and impact of organizational communication has grown exponentially. In this chapter, the ability to leverage the value of organizational communication is explored through the concept of an organization's rhetorical consciousness. This concept advances the interplay between an organization and its approach to communication beyond what Ruth C. Smith identifies as structural ("containment"), coproduced ("production"), or isomorphic ("equivalency") paradigms[1] (qtd. in Putnam, Phillips & Chapman, 1996, p. 375). The discussion of a rhetorical consciousness offers a way of engaging organizational communication as a catalyst for dynamic, ethical communicative exchange for both internal and external audiences. Specifically, this discussion considers the rhetorical consciousness of an organization as a means of engendering story-centered engagement. Framed with Calvin O. Schrag's (1986) conception of "communicative praxis"[2]—communication about something, by someone, and for someone—the notion of a rhetorical consciousness provides a hermeneutic entrance for understanding the purpose of organizational communication as more than communication of a brand or integrated messages. It pushes beyond process to story-centered engagement that culminates in an ethical challenge: to think carefully about the story of an organization because it impacts people, not just because it impacts purchases, product launches, or quarterly reports.

Understood vis-à-vis a praxis framework, the rhetorical consciousness of an organization is constituted in the interplay of communication about an organization and its product(s) and/or service(s), by embedded constituents (especially marketers), for a given audience(s) as a means by which the invention, creation, implementation, and lived experience of the organization might be understood as well as storied. More than integration of key messages toward the establishment or reinforcement of a brand, or integration based in emotional connections, a concept embodied in what Kevin Roberts (2004) calls a "lovemark,"[3] the guiding presupposition of this discussion is that through communication to its various constituents, organizations impact human experience. More specifically, organizations impact the way in which people story[4] their existence.

In terms of communicative engagement, organizations assist in the creation of commonplaces that enable people to connect, share their experiences, and story their individual and collective existence. By focusing on the praxis nature of organizational rhetorical consciousness, this chapter situates the internal and external formation of an organizational story within communication—within the multiplicity and variety of meaningful ways in which people communicate, share experiences, and conduct their lives. Through the idea of living "*in* communication," the impact of organizational communication is directly linked to what the organization is as well as to its impact on people, society, and culture (Carey, 1989). The rhetorical consciousness thus becomes the background from which communicative coherence might be established and meaningful participation engendered.

At the core of an organization's rhetorical consciousness is "ownership"[5] of the organization in such a way that people can do as Jeff Bezos, founder and CEO of Amazon.com, suggests. In an interview with Alan Deutschman (2004) of *Fast Company*, Bezos said the following about the importance of organizational purpose and communication of that purpose, "You can hold a rock concert and that can be successful, and you can hold a ballet and that can be successful, but don't hold a rock concert and advertise it as a ballet. If you're very clear to the outside world...then people can self-select in" (p. 58). The coherent framing of an organization, what it stands for, offers, and even asks of those who associate with it allows people to self-select in and remain a part of the organization over the long term. As such, it points toward what Lowe, Carr, Thomas, and Watkins-Mathys (2005) advance as the "fourth hermeneutic in marketing theory": the "slowing down of frenetic consumption" through the adoption of "moral artistry" grounded in a value-dimension in and through which organizational life might be constituted (pp. 198-199). A developed approach to communicative action constituted from within a value-dimension of organizational life is vital to addressing what Lowe et al. (2005) identify as a "clear and pressing demand" in this historical moment (p. 198): the need for a shift in communicative practices toward a "value reflexive and processual dialectical orientation" and away from practices that fail to consider the implications of organizational communication in fostering particular views of consumption (p. 199). More than simply integrating communication for coherence and consistency in internal and external messaging, the value reflexive and processual dialectical orientation draws attention to the relevance of wisdom, morality, spirit, and soul to "balance knowledge and transcend its inherent limitations" (p. 197).

Although this chapter does not directly address these sensibilities, it does offer the rhetorical consciousness of an organization as a way of constituting the communicative background from which ethical decisions might be made. As a praxis form of interaction, the rhetorical consciousness of an organization necessitates consideration of multiple perspectives. In this way, a rhetorical consciousness speaks to the practical wisdom, or phronesis, needed to comprehend the world, as well as the exercise of this wisdom in the ongoing life of society (Schrag, 1986). In the spirit of Putnam et al.'s (1996) work on "metaphors of communication and organization," the rhetorical consciousness of an organization does not place the organization in the "role of *figure* or principal subject" although communication assumes a secondary role but within an understanding of "communication as the producer of organizations" (p. 376). As such, the praxis nature of rhetorical consciousness can therefore best be viewed as forming the life of an organization in and through a communicative interplay. The result is a communicative gestalt in which engagement about, by, and for produces a story compelling enough for people to self-select in.

In the following pages, the communicative metaphor of a rhetorical consciousness is framed through an articulation of the importance of a praxis approach to organizational communication in this historical moment followed by the explication of its three foundational praxis coordinates: (1) communication about something as purposeful organizational communication about an organization and its product(s) and/or service(s), (2) communication *by* someone as the communicative call of those embedded within an organization (notably marketers), and (3) communication for others as communication toward specific communities of conversation (audience[s]). In the intertexture of communication about, by and for, this chapter suggests that organizational communication becomes a storied phenomenon whereby meaning is created and shared experiences are made possible. More than a process, the concept of a rhetorical consciousness of an organization is a communicative framework through which organizational communication might confidently apply, not rely on processes, and move into the realm of dynamic communicative exchange through story-centered engagement.

From "Integration" to Communication: The Imperative of This Historical Moment

The praxis engagement of a rhetorical consciousness is responsive to the reality that the corporate identity landscape continues to "become more active and crowded" (Balmer & Greyser, 2003,

p. 15). It is not surprising that what is "germane to conceiving what it means to be human"—identity—is also "central to the conceptualization of one of the most complex and fascinating of human creations, the work organization" (Dennis A. Gioia qtd. in Balmer & Greyser, 2003, p. 31). In fact, the proliferation of mergers, acquisitions, reimaging, rebranding, and technological advances make the importance of safeguarding organizational identity more salient than ever. Like the cultivation of individual identity, "who" owns an organization becomes paramount to establishing its place in the marketplace. Moreover, ownership is essential to establishing connections, relevance, and ultimately long-term relationships with customers.

In recent decades, a driving imperative in response to the demands of ownership on organizational identity formation has been "integration," specifically integrated marketing communication. In a summary work aiming at a new definition of integrated marketing communication, Jerry Kliatchko (2005) reinforces what has been the case since the public introduction of integration: there is still no consensus on the scope or general concept of integrated marketing communication. To overview the commonly accepted perspectives on integrated marketing communication, Kliatchko identifies five seminal definitions ranging from integration as the nurturing of relationships to integration as the coordination of messages to integration as a strategic process. The culmination of the chapter is in Kliatchko's own definition: an "audience-focused, channel-centered, and results-driven" approach to integrated marketing communication (p. 31).

As with many of the other definitions, Kliatchko's (2005) fusion privileges attributes that are still reliant on processes, most notably those that are quantifiable. The questions guiding integrated marketing communication and integration more broadly, however, are reminiscent of the direction of Lowe et al. (2005) regarding the fourth hermeneutic, suggesting that there are certain qualities that cannot be codified into a process or statistical rendering of behaviors. Regarding these types of questions, responses by the various integrated marketing schools of thought converge around a theme: a "back to basics" movement geared toward reflexivity and continued development of marketing to meet the challenges of today's marketplace (Brown, 1997, p. 168). This theme is characterized by the "development of ultra-modern but nostalgically styled 'retro' products, advertising or retailing environments" (Brown, 1997, p. 167). It recognizes that in high-tech industries where discontinuous innovation is the norm, alternative means are required for "crossing the chasm" and reaching potential as well as actual markets (Brown, 1997, p. 167; Moore, 1991, p. 35). Back to basics is a theme that acknowledges modern marketing's pursuit of scientific accuracy as validation for its theoretical prowess, as well as accommodates the postmodern questioning of scientific methodologies and the mantra of progress dueling for ascendancy in the "Is marketing an art or science?" debate (Brown, 1997, p. 168).

Despite the momentum gained through conversations around integration and getting back to the basics, the postmodern marketplace continues to demand clarity and nimbleness from marketing that has yet to be delivered through the "process" of integration as it is currently envisioned and employed. The questioning of integration in this historical moment boldly invites a more textured and holistic approach to marketing theory and practice that recognizes more fully the communicative, storied nature of life. As a vehicle for stimulating connections between organizations, products, and particular markets, the communicative importance of marketing moves beyond integration to an understanding of the ability of organizational communication, marketing or otherwise, to help "story" a necessary strand in every human being's "web of significance"[6] (Geertz, 1973, p. 5).

The prophetic insights of Walter Benjamin's (1986) 1936 essay "The Storyteller" foreshadows the need for greater attentiveness to the storied nature of human existence as he laments an impending crisis in our ability to exchange experiences–what he calls a crisis in the art of storytelling. In his essay, Benjamin (1986) analyzes the rise in value of information qua information and the subsequent cultural focus on "abbreviation" and "prompt verifiability" over the craft of telling and retelling experience (pp. 89, 93). He believes that the crisis in the art of storytelling is reaching its end as "the epic side of truth, wisdom, is dying out" (Benjamin, 1986, p. 87). It follows from his argument that information processed for the sake of information inhibits the sharing of experience and the continuance of "living traditions"–traditions that form the larger history within which current experiences are embedded and made intelligible (MacIntyre, 1984, p. 222). The whole of Benjamin's critique points toward the increasing difficulty in weaving shared webs of significance between people across generations and cultures.

In Volume 2 of his *Time and Narrative* series, Paul Ricoeur (1985) considers Benjamin's critique of storytelling as an indictment of a market-driven culture, specifically advertising's role and influence in it. Ricoeur (1985) states that "perhaps we are at the end of an era where narrating no longer has a place...because human beings no longer have any experience to share. And he [Benjamin] sees in the rule of advertising the sign of this retreat of narrative, a retreat without return" (p. 228). According to Benjamin's (1986) critique, advertising's role in a market-driven culture is to provide information that is "understandable in itself" for dissemination in the moment (p. 89). The communicative value of a focus on information in the moment is in the ability to control distance and people through effectively transmitted messages (Carey, 1989, p. 15). In this surrender to abbreviation, it would seem that advertising's ability to be associated with the craft of storytelling–a craft that draws from the past, speaks to the present, and is attentive to the future–is a stretch, at best. Benjamin's critique of advertising—the most visible sign of marketing and its discontents in popular culture—questions the whole of marketing as well. Simply stated, Ricoeur's interpretation of Benjamin presents an indictment of marketing as putting at risk our ability to story our own existence.

From this point of concern, the imperative to "integrate" and its process-oriented conceptualizations aimed at identity development and maintenance are ill-equipped to recapture what Benjamin and Ricoeur view as lost or seriously jeopardized. A focus on communication, specifically its storied nature and its ability to "narrate the organization,"[7] begins to open the possibility of reclaiming shared experiences and subsequently the ability of people living in and engaging a particular historical moment to establishing meaning, connect, and story their existence. To understand the importance of organizational identity beyond integration is to understand an organization's inextricable relationship with communication, specifically the ability to establish purposeful meanings, as well as meaningful connections in and through communication.

James Twitchell's (1999) statement on popular culture points to the significance of organizational communication as it impacts people: it "is simply impossible to consume objects without consuming meaning. Meaning is pumped and drawn everywhere throughout the modern commercial world" (p. 283). To this point, Twitchell

(1999) argues that the "consumption of things and their meanings is how most Western young people cope in a world that science has pretty much bled of traditional religious meanings" (p. 12). It follows from Twitchell's observation that marketplace organizations inherit a position of responsibility not traditionally theirs. Although not fully abandoning the directed nature of Twitchell's argument, the importance of his insight for this chapter is in the recognition of the communicative impact that organizations—secular and religious, for-profit and not-for-profit alike—have on interactions between people in the formation of shared experiences, personal stories, society, and culture. The bottom line is that as communication is developed to make connections between an organization's products and/or services and people's everyday lives, meaning is created, lives are impacted, and culture is changed.

In his work, *Communication as Culture: Essays on Media and Society,* communication scholar James Carey (1989) makes the imperative of this communication-marketplace connection explicit. The catalyst for his writing is the presupposition that we live in communication— in "dramatic action" as participants in culture; we are not simply passive recipients (Carey, 1989, p. 45). To this end, communication is more than the transmission of information as a means to control distance and people. "Communication as culture" is also about a more "ritualistic" understanding of communication: "the maintenance of society in time" (Carey, 1989, p. 18). It is not about the act of "imparting information" but about how people represent their shared beliefs (p. 18). Therefore communication as culture endows organizations with a deeper purpose—the creation of commonplaces that people connect with and through as they story their lives.

A more specific application of this idea is found in *The World of Goods: Towards an Anthropology of Consumption.* In this work, anthropologist Mary Douglas and economist Baron Isherwood (1979) challenge the patronizing literature on consumption that degrades people's attempts to consume at the same level as their friends ("keeping up with the Joneses"), offering instead a perspective that views consumption as a way to relate to others. In light of a breakdown in the traditional forms of community, Douglas and Isherwood's (1979) research leads to the idea that individuals are "freed" in consumption to engage in new rituals of exchange—consumption rituals—to "make sense" of life (p. xxii, 40). This process of exchange is driven by a different sense of community-consumers who need to "be included meaningfully with fellow consumers" (Douglas & Isherwood, 1979, p. 118). Goods, as "ritual adjuncts," are thus an essential part of "mak[ing] sense of the inchoate flux of events" that is a part of everyday life (p. 43); they help to bring order and sense-making to disparate experiences. Consumption rituals, like rituals in general, "serve to contain the drift of [shared] meanings" thereby providing a common point of association for people (p. 43). Ultimately, these rituals help to define the conventions that provide people with public definitions within which to communicate and experience life.

The philosophical and pragmatic importance of Douglas and Isherwood's (1979) insights is in their overt gesturing toward a crucial point of convergence between consumer society and organizational identity formation–a point at the heart of the communicative imperative for this historical moment: the search for concordance that is the aspiring nature of all human communication. For Paul Ricoeur (1984), the search for concordance is a "part of the unavoidable assumptions of discourse and communication" (p. 28). It is characterized by "completeness, wholeness, and an appropriate magnitude" (p. 38). In terms of organizations and their communication, these characteristics invite a multilayered commitment by the organization to its own purpose and vision, about the benefits of the brand, both real and perceived, and to "the intelligent use of action" for a particular audience (p. 40). The search for concordance is a position whereby the organization is aware of its existence in relation to itself and simultaneously aware of itself in relation to others. Identity is not an isolated phenomenon, but as Putnam et al. (1996) and Czarniawska (1997) suggest, it is something that is aspired to, performed, engaged, and developed in conversation with others.

The shift from an imperative of integration to one of communication, specifically concordance through communication, calls attention to the salient demands of this historical moment. In one sense, its universal claim demystifies the trendy approaches to safeguarding organizational identity through brand or emotional lovemarks. At the same time, it invigorates an understanding of communicative exchange grounded in connections and shared experiences that inform the way in which communication works to story human existence, the basis of which is achieved in identity. The communicative imperative of concordance enables "creative imitation" at all levels of identity formation though the attention is on discovering and interpreting the connections in people's lives, connections noted as being embedded in experience and not on replicating a process for adherence (Ricoeur, 1984, p. 31). For organizations, the communicative imperative of concordance in this historical moment demands more than marketing can offer in terms of integration, strategic objective setting, or return on investment; it demands more than an approach to organizational communication derived from a prescribed paradigm. Concordance extends the conversation related to organizational communication in such a way as to remind us that ownership is achieved in the interplay of communicative connections, not in the premeditated implementation of processes employed as means to specified ends.

Rhetorical Consciousness as Communicative Praxis

As explored in the earlier section, the communicative imperative of this historical moment calls for an engagement of the storied nature of human existence—the way in which we share our experiences, shape our lives, and influence the world in which we live—that concordance might be made possible. The communicative metaphor of a rhetorical consciousness within an organization is offered here as a way of framing organizational communication from the inside-out so as to enhance the possibility of internal and external constituents being able to self-select in, thereby increasing the likelihood of concordant associations. The underlying premise is that ownership begins internally with owning the "who" of an organization. Communicative praxis as a framework for conceiving rhetorical consciousness engenders practical wisdom on the part of organizations to assert this ownership that self-selection might be a normative point of departure.

In the following pages, Schrag's threefold hermeneutic of communication praxis (about, by, and for someone) is briefly examined and connected to organizational communication. Broadly conceived, the nature of Schrag's (1986) threefold hermeneutic is the engagement of discourse and action as being "*about* something, by someone, *for* someone. Communicative praxis thus displays a referential moment (about a world of human concerns and social practices), a moment of self-implicature (by a speaker, author, or actor), and a rhetorical moment (directedness to the other)" (Schrag, 1986, p. viii). In *The Resources of Rationality,* Schrag (1992) elaborates on communicative praxis this way.

This wider space of communicative praxis is proposed as a displacement of the ethereal metaphysical regions of the ancients as well as the narrow epistemological straits of the moderns. It is within this new space of inquiry, post-metaphysical and post-epistemological, that rationality undergoes its recovery and the workings of the dialectics of participation and distanciation become manifest.... [The] recovery of the space of communicative praxis restores the dense network of we-relationships that supplies the binding topos of rhetoric.... It is illustrated by the reciprocity of social interaction.... [Communicative praxis is] a network of interdependencies, involving the rhetor, the audience, and the ethos of the tradition in which both stand. (pp. 64, 130-131)

Schrag's about, by, and for establish communicative praxis as responsive engagement in everyday life. The interplay of these produces a holistic phenomenon—"a shared project and a joint endeavor by a community of investigators and interpreters" (Schrag, 1986, p. 190)–that acknowledges a multiplicity of forms of discourse and action situated against the background of tradition (Schrag, 1992, p. 166).

The specific framing of each coordinate begins with an explication vis-à-vis the work of Schrag followed immediately by a connection of the praxis coordinates to communication within organizations. What is ultimately depicted in the interplay of communication about, by, and for is the creation of a relationship that is unitary yet multifaceted. The three coordinates are independent of one another in form, yet interconnected in terms of their communicative impact. The rhetorical consciousness of an organization as communicative praxis is then discussed according to this interplay in what the concluding section identifies as communication for story-centered engagement.

Communication "about" an Organization and Its Products and/or Services

The "about" of communicative praxis establishes the texts of human experience as varied—for example, gestures, words, habits, customs, written texts, and visual texts are all included. It is a holistic, gestalt understanding of action and experience that does not function in a reactive capacity, but seeks, instead, to provide insight into what has been said and done to facilitate "critical, discerning reflection and creative, inventive insight" about something in a particular historical moment (Schrag, 1986, p. 110).

Rather than contriving an abstract rendering or simply disregarding its presence, Schrag (1986) underscores the importance of the historical moment as one of human experience (p. 60). From this understanding, communication about something is opened as "referential"—a "recollecting forward"—in which history and temporality are commingled (p. 70). The combined movements of distance (the experience regarding history) and reflection (the ability to focus in temporality) open the space of communicative praxis "for a fusion and redescription of the varied configurations of discourse and action" against which meaning might be established (p. 71).

According to Schrag (1986), the establishment of meaning and meaningful connections is experienced in relations between "self and society, the individual and the collective, man and his institutions" (p. 206). In these relations, the dialectic of participation and distanciation or distance in a given historical moment produces a "transversal interplay" (Schrag, 1992, p. 63). Transversality allows for a more comprehensive examination of human experience, drawing attention to an understanding of this experience as situated "intercommunally" in the world (p. 64); one cannot escape another. The ability to engage the dialectic of participation and distance enables moments of critical reflection from which insight might be gained and applied to overall participation in the shared human experience. In the space of communicative praxis, the transversal interplay announces the intersection of multiple experiences, and helps to contend against blind traditionalism and the "tyranny of custom" that inhibit the interplay of these in everyday life.

Communicative praxis about something speaks to action and experience that is situated and understood in context. In the communicative life of an organization, internal and external, the "about something" refers to the public centrality of goods to the storied nature of human existence. Through the referential reality of goods, this praxis coordinate pushes organizational communication beyond the current scope of integration to an engagement of it as communicative content through what can be called "the truth-value of the proposition" (Schrag, 1992, p. 56). Highlighting what is and is not offered–presenting the truth value of a good—is not about maximizing short-term profitability, providing a quick fix, or pushing a way of life on people. As the substantive content of organizational communication, the about something shifts "process" toward "purpose" and the consideration of organizational communication as it assists in the formation of meaning in people's lives–how it nurtures "multiple ways, some new and some old, of interpreting the world and acting within it" (Schrag, 1986, p. 115). In this way, it is understood that "all goods carry meaning, but none by itself" (Douglas & Isherwood, 1979, p. 49). This moves the neutrality of an organization and its goods (products and/or services) to a more realistic examination of them as part of a dynamic and culturally relevant relationship–as part of the stories that are woven together to form people's webs of significance.

Communication "by" an Embedded Marketer

Within the threefold hermeneutic of communicative praxis, communication about something is always done by someone. In *The Self after Postmodernity,* Schrag (1997) makes the following declaration regarding the praxis-oriented subject.

> In the aftermath of the deconstruction of traditional metaphysics and epistemology, a new self emerges, like a phoenix arising from its ashes—a praxis-oriented self, defined by its communicative practices, oriented toward an understanding of itself in its discourse, its action, its being with others, and its experience of transcendence. The narration of this story of self-understanding is scripted as a response both to the discourse of modernity and to the postmodern challenge, addressing the roles of the culture-spheres of science, morality, art, religion in their functions of defining the sociohistorical process of self-formation. (p. 9)

Schrag's (1986) theory of communicative praxis seeks to reclaim the "who" of action from "solipsistic volitional intentions" into a space in which every individual action encompasses

> the social practices of other agents and actors and formative influences that issue from them. This conditions every individual action by the acting subject as a response to a previous action.... The trace of subjectivity in individual decision and action thus furrows a path to configurations of shared experiences and joint endeavors. (p. 135)

Encountering the other leads to an "epistemological rupture"— a questioning of the absolute presence of the self as constituting the entirety of experience (Schrag, 1986, p. 136). In this rupture, the subject is deconstructed and restored "as speaker, author, and actor [sic] not as a foundation for communicative praxis but as an implicate of it" (p. 138).

The restored subject is "decentered"—characterized as embodied, a phenomenon of varying profiles temporally situated (Schrag, 1986, p. 145, 149). Embodiment recasts the meaning of "presence" as the expression of bodily gestures and considers these "events of hermeneutical disclosure" (p. 153). Multiplicity challenges theoretical professions of ontological or epistemic certainty, offering, instead, the subject as part of an ongoing conversation through which its identity is shaped. Finally, in a radical critique of temporality communicative praxis permits the "play of presence with absence.... The presence of the subject is a living present, coming from a past and projecting into a future. As such it is the enabling of repetition and anticipation, preservation and creation, conservation and invention" (p. 146).

Communication by someone in an organization is about the communicative call of a marketer or other embedded agent(s) within a given organization whose "embodied" commitment requires more than the integration of communication processes for the end goal of selling "stuff." Embedded within the communicative life of an organization and its associated goods—in a "history of language and social practices"—organizational communication by someone begins with the public acknowledgment of presuppositions and a given standpoint[8] that exist because of this embeddedness (Schrag, 1986, p. 176). Story-centered engagement is developed through this public acknowledgment and the concomitant hermeneutical responsibility of the embedded marketer to both the organization and its audiences.

The embedded marketer is one who interprets and communicates ideas that are specific to a given organization and its products and/or services that understanding might be established and meaning emerge between people as they participate in the multiplicity of everyday life, the communicative dynamics of the organization, and the public nature of good(s) and/or service(s). The interpretive role of the embedded marketer implicates their role within the dynamics of a communicative sphere in which it is coconstituted "with other subjects as the narrator, actor, and respondent within the human drama of discourse and social practices" (Schrag, 1986, p. 138). In creating understanding, the marketer invites people into a conversation already begun, with the possibility of participation and belonging formed within a specific community of conversation. Communication by someone thus positions the call of an embedded marketer and/or other embedded agent(s) as one of building and maintaining trust through interpretation and the clear communication of the truth-value of the good so that understanding can be publicly realized.

Communication "for" Communities of Conversation

The third feature of communicative praxis is inextricably linked to the other two. Communication about something, by someone, is inherently *for* another. According to Schrag, the disclosure of the other "is generalized to encompass the hearer in the dialogic transaction, the audience of a public assembly, the reader of a text, and the respondent citizen in the polis of praxis-oriented existence" (Schrag, 1986, p. 179). In making a turn toward the other, communicative praxis takes on a rhetorical dimension that encompasses more fully human potentiality and the human condition.

In the space of communicative praxis, discourse and action toward someone is not synonymous with manipulation or technique-driven practices. Communication for someone is explicitly ethical—"an indelible feature of the creation and preservation of meaning" (Schrag, 1986, p. 180). With foundations in the rhetorical tradition of Aristotle, communication for another establishes discourse, art, and persuasion as working together to establish common ground among audience members and between the audience and rhetor, as well as to call the hearers to responsible judgment and action. According to Schrag (1986), the linkage of rhetoric to a hermeneutic of everyday life reinforces a wider horizon[9] of communicative praxis from which to disclose the "possibilities for agreed upon perspectives on seeing the world and the acting within it" (p. 187).

In the realm of organizational communication, being for someone is not about privileging a consumer perspective nor is it a means to purchasing consumers on the basis of behavioral predictability studies. Organizational communication for someone is a response to the need for a broader communicative perspective through the act of being-for-others as they exist in communities of conversation. The communicative thrust of marketing for someone is constituted in a consciousness toward the other whereby discourse and action toward or for someone is not viewed as the "manipulation of propositions" toward an ideological end but as part of the "hermeneutic of everyday life, where truth is more a matter of disclosure than correspondence" (Schrag, 1986, p. 187).

For embedded marketers, communities of conversation provide the ethos or "dwelling" space of (moral) discourse and action in which the self is implicated and the other disclosed (Schrag, 1986, p. 202). In these communicative spheres, people live, share experiences, and story what it means to be human. Communities of conversation are, therefore, an ethical space of engagement in which the invitation of understanding is made. Organizational communication for someone is thus an act of being-for-others, a response to the moral dimension of the communicative spaces (communities of conversation) that shape people's lives.

Rhetorical Consciousness as Ethical Communicative Engagement

Schrag's theory of communicative praxis offers a framework for organizational communication that is constituted in and through responsive discourse and action in everyday life. In response to the imperative of this historical moment, the praxis of organizational rhetorical consciousness builds on attempts at coherence and consistency through integration to better address what Ricoeur (1984) identifies as the driving force of all communication—the search for concordance. Concordance is not about "sameness," but about the "synthesis of the heterogeneous" (Ricoeur, 1984, p. 66). The praxis nature of rhetorical consciousness as conceived in this chapter is able to respond to the contingencies and embedded nature of lived experience by offering a framework that helps articulate the need for people to connect and "grasp together" multiple and varied experiences into something coherent, even if the point of convergence and understanding is through organizations not traditionally associated with having a significant role in the formation of meaning and shared experiences.

Where integration through integrated marketing communication sought to align communication around audience, through channels, and/or in terms of results, a communication praxis approach recognizes more fully the communicative, storied nature of human existence. It is this distinction that invites consideration of the rhetorical consciousness of an organization as ethical communicative engagement. Through the interrelation of communication about an organization and its products and/or services, by an embedded marketer, for communities of conversation (audience[s]) in a given historical moment, the praxis nature of an organization's rhetorical consciousness is, according to Schrag (1986), a hermeneutic that guides the construction of a "fitting response"—the response of the decentered subject "in its encounter with the discourse and social practices of the other against the backdrop of the delivered tradition" (p. 202).

A fitting response is being attentive to the impact of the past, the present, and the future on the historical moment. It grasps the present moment as inherently ethical–one of responsibility, deliberation, and action (Schrag, 1986, p. 207). The past is recollected, providing the means by which discourse and social practices are preserved. Finally, the future is anticipated as the realm of new possibilities for redescription and reinterpretation.

The about, by, and for of an organization's rhetorical consciousness form an interpretive horizon from which the applicability of goods, invitation to participation, and audiences are made visible for interpretation, understanding, and invitation. All along this horizon is a multiplicity of opportunities out of which might be established a "fitting" or appropriate response to communicative demands in a given historical moment. Ethical engagement thus begins with the interplay of communication about, by, and for something oriented toward a purposeful "fit" reminiscent of Jeff Bezos' commentary on establishing meaningful and relevant connections through clarity of organizational ownership. To this goal, communication "about something" marks a commitment to an understanding of goods as commonplaces. The about something of an organization truly situates ownership of organizational identity from the inside-out vis-à-vis the truth-value and public nature of goods. Communication "by someone" in an organization is a "calling out" of an embedded marketer in the organization as well as in the historical moment to interpret what is being offered in such a way as to engender understanding and invite people to participate in a conversation that is already under way. Thus, communicating "for someone"—the third and final coordinate—is an invitation. It is the rhetorical action of being-for-the-other in communities of conversation formed as a by-product of exchange. These communities inhabit a distinctly moral space–a space that influences the way in which they choose and use goods to story their individual and collective existence.

Together, the about, by, and for of a praxis framework for the rhetorical consciousness of an organization acknowledges the imperative of concordance as defining this historical moment. In the spirit of Putnam et al. (1996), communication produces an organization as well as the shared experiences and storied existences emergent from association in or with that organization. As a praxis mode of engagement, the rhetorical consciousness works within the horizon of that organization to employ communication in such a way that people choose to self-select in. The ethical engagement is not inspired by adherence to codes or processes, but by inviting ownership through story-centered engagement grounded in a textured commitment to multiple goods in a given historical moment.

As indicated throughout, story-centered engagement is the by-product of an organization's rhetorical conscious in action. Within the praxis interplay of an organization's rhetorical consciousness, the framework for organizational communication is textured by an attentiveness to the way in which people connect and story their lives, as well as to the role of an organization in cultivating these stories and impacting people, society, and culture across generations. In doing so, the rhetorical consciousness of an organization points toward the possibility of genuine meeting between an organization and people as they story their everyday experiences. It suggests the possibility of meeting people in such a way that they self-select in to the organization, whether in terms of their time, talent, or financial resources. Working from the inside-out, a rhetorical consciousness facilitates story-centered engagement and participatory decision making inspired by invitation. As such, a rhetorical consciousness provides a framework for organizational communication in which the point of departure for internal and external communication is not integrated processes, but ownership of the organization and its story.

Notes

1   The original distinctions between these three ways of understanding the relationship between an organization and communication can be found in Ruth C. Smith's paper "Images of organizational communication: Root-metaphors of the organization-communication relation" presented at the 1993 International Communication Association Conference in Washington, D.C.

2   The use of "about," "by," and "for" throughout this document are tied explicitly to Calvin O. Schrag's work, *Communicative Praxis and the Space of Subjectivity*. As prepositional terms, they are found in part and whole in various other communication related works, however, none explicate them in the same way as Schrag. Therefore, the author of this chapter attributes all references of these terms only to Schrag.

3   According to Roberts (2004), "lovemarks" are the result of a strong and

emotional connection between people and the things that they are passionate about. More information can be obtained in Roberts's book *Lovemarks: The Future Beyond Brands* (powerHouse Books in April of 2004 and then again in 2005).

4   The idea of storying one's existence is referenced here in the spirit of both Walter Fisher and Alasdair MacIntyre's more encompassing understanding of narrative as foundational to the way in which we comprehend and engage life. In this context, to story one's life encompasses discrete moments as well as the gestalt picture of one's lived experience.

5   Ownership is applied here in accordance with F. Byron Nahser's "own who you are" concept as developed in his work *Learning to Read the Signs: Reclaiming Pragmatism in Business*, published in 1997 by Boston-based Butterworth-Heinemann.

6   "Web of significance" is a term adapted by cultural anthropologist Clifford Geertz (1973) from the writings of Max Weber. It refers to culture as "interworked systems of construable signs" (p. 12)-a public context that people act in and on. It is "not an experimental science in search of law but an interpretive one in search of meaning" (p. 5). For more, see Geertz (1973, pp. 5-24).

7   The idea of narrating the organization is referenced here in relation to Barbara Czarniawska's (1997) approach to understanding the "forms in which knowledge is cast" within organizations (p. 6). Central to her work is a view of science as a conversation and the "process of storytelling as the never-ending construction of meaning in organizations" (p. 28). For more, consult Czarniawska, B. (1997).

8   For the purposes of this work, "standpoint" is used within the purview of standpoint theory and is synonymous with references to the embedded nature of people's lives. As in standpoint theory, it adds an individual's situatedness to a cultural perspective, referring to the fact that a person experiences and engages life from a particular position within culture framed by who they are, what they believe, and the circumstances that shape their life. According to standpoint theory, this includes contributing factors such as gender, ethnicity, socioeconomic influence, as well as religious and professional orientation. The origins of this theory are tied to German philosopher Georg Wilhelm Friedrich Hegel's 1807 work Phenomenology of mind. In Sandra Harding's contemporary reflections on standpoint, the development of the theory is furthered through a focus on the limitations of people's situatedness and the implications of these limits on a person's mobility within a hierarchy of social life. For more information, see Harding, S. (1991).

9   Horizon is tied to Gadamer's (1998) conception of a "historically effected consciousness." A horizon provides parameters or guidelines within which to work and adapt. It makes visible the present and the background against which the present is situated. A given horizon refers to the "range of vision that includes everything that can be seen from a particular vantage point" (p. 302). For more, see Gadamer, H.G. (1998).

References

Balmer, J. M.T., & Greyser, S. A. (2003). Managing the multiple identities of the corporation. Revealing the corporation: Perspectives on identity, image, reputation, corporate branding, and corporate-level marketing. New York: Routledge. 15-29.

Benjamin, W. (1986). The storyteller. (H. Zohn, Trans.). Illuminations: Walter Benjamin, essays and reflections. (H. Arendt, Ed.). New York: Schocken Books. (Original work published 1936). 83-109.

Brown, S. (1997). Marketing science in a postmodern world: Introduction to the special issue. *European Journal of Marketing*, 31 (3/4), 167-182.

Carey, J. (1989). Communications as culture: Essays on media and society. New York: Routledge.

Czarniawska, B. (1997). Narrating the organization: Dramas of institutional identity. Chicago: University of Chicago Press.

Deutschman, A. (2004, August). Inside the mind of Jeff Bezos. *Fast Company*, 85, 52.

Douglas, M. & Isherwood, B. (1979). The world of goods: Towards an anthropology of consumption. London: Routledge.

Gadamer, H. (1998). Truth and method. (Joel Weinsheimer & Donald G. Marshall, Trans., 2nd rev. ed.). New York: Continuum.

Geertz, C. (1973). Interpretation of cultures. New York: Basic Books.

Kliatchko, J. (2005). Towards a new definition of integrated marketing communications (IMC). *International Journal of Advertising*, 24 (1), 7-34.

Lowe, S., Carr, A. N., Thomas, M., & Watkins-Mathys, L. (2005). The fourth hermeneutic in marketing theory. *Marketing Theory*, 5 (2), 185-203.

MacIntyre, A. (1984). After virtue: A study in moral theory (2nd ed.). Notre Dame, IN: University of Notre Dame Press.

Moore, G. A. (1991). Crossing the chasm: Marketing and selling high tech products to mainstream consumers. New York: HarperBusiness.

Nahser, F. B. (1997). Learning to read the signs: Reclaiming pragmatism in business. Boston: Butterworth-Heinemann.

Putnam, L., Phillips, N., & Chapman, P. (1996). Metaphors of communication and organization. In S. R. Clegg, C. Hardy, & W. R. Nord (Eds.), Handbook of organization studies (pp. 375-408). Thousand Oaks, CA: Sage.

Ricoeur, P. (1984). Time and narrative: Volume 1. (K. McLaughlin & D. Pellauer, Trans.). Chicago: University of Chicago Press.

———. (1985). Time and narrative: Volume 2. (K. McLaughlin & D. Pellauer, Trans.). Chicago: University of Chicago Press.

Roberts, K. (2004). Lovemarks: The future beyond brands. New York: powerHouse Books.

Schrag, C. O. (1986). Communicative praxis and the space of subjectivity. Bloomington: Indiana University Press.

———. (1992). The resources of rationality: A response to the postmodern challenge. Bloomington: Indiana University Press.

———. (1997). The self after postmodernity. New Haven, CT: Yale University Press.

Twitchell, J. B. (1999). Lead us into temptation: The triumph of American materialism. New York: Columbia University Press.

Conclusion

Ronald C. Arnett

I am honored to offer an afterword to this important work, *Philosophies of Communication: Implications for Everyday Experience*. My gratitude rests with the conviction that this project contributes to an increasingly important area of communication study—the philosophy of communication. In addition, I am grateful that Michael Hyde wrote the foreword. Michael's work is an exemplar of the pragmatic insightfulness discerned through the study and application of the philosophy of communication. Both this project and Michael's astute long-standing scholarly contributions offer a clarion announcement that trumpets the importance of the philosophy of communication for discovering temporal clarity in an era defined by difference.

Introduction

The notion of an "afterword" provides opportunity for continuing the conversation about the philosophy of communication in everyday life. The implications of "what is next" begins with an examination of the title of this work, moves to discussion of the heuristic insights of each chapter, and ends with a genuine expression of "bravo" for the diversity of this discipline and the possibilities for future projects in philosophy of communication.

This moment, often labeled "postmodernity," is an era defined by difference; it is an era in which awareness about differences between persons rests at the forefront of communicative life. Even calls suggesting that "postmodernity" is dead and that narrative conformity has once again arisen with hegemonic influence remind us not of the truism of conformity, but of differences among us in the reading of this historical moment. When evidence for conformity rests within the initial reaction to 9/11, one must ask whether such uniformity is still in place. The answer is a resounding "no." We live in an era of competing narrative and virtue structures. Philosophy of communication assists in discerning what might be the appropriate reaction to a particular difference in a given historical moment.

The remainder of this afterword outlines the connection between philosophy of communication and difference, the heuristic implications of chapters that compose this fine volume, and a concluding bravo for their future work and, of course, the discipline.

Philosophy of Communication as Difference

Richard Bernstein (1983) was correct—we find ourselves in a peculiar moment in which the philosophical and the pragmatic have crisscrossed. In this historical moment, it is pragmatic to learn about philosophies of communication that assist us in learning and understanding the differences that shape everyday existence. Philosophies of communication help us discern the significance of the everyday in an era of competing narrative and virtue structures.

Difference once was primarily the province of intercultural communication. This insight continues rightly to push the ongoing study of difference between cultures with increasing attentiveness to differences in religion, culture, governance, race, ethnicity, and affectivity entering the conversation about difference in intercultural communication studies.

Today difference is increasingly a normative assumption no longer tied to lack of proximity alone. Today one finds difference in the conceptual space between neighbors, friends, and within families. What is new in the realm of difference is not intercultural cultural awareness, but attentiveness to difference in the everyday. We need not turn to places of great distance to find difference. Difference is now a driving reality between friends, families, and neighbors. Difference is still the province of intercultural communication, but it is no longer the sole placeholder of the study of difference.

Philosophy of communication is now the intercultural communication activity of the everyday—assisting with knowledge and understanding of differences. Intercultural communication and philosophy of communication both seek to understand difference, the alterity of presuppositions between persons far from one another physically and those walking in the same house and conceptually far from one another.

The insights of Clifford Geertz (1973) and "concepts near" and "concepts far" display the power of anthropology in the understanding of another culture, being the way of engagement of a member of a community and an outside scholar, respectively. Geertz displayed the importance of vision tempered by ideas, theories, and insight propelled by experience from the outside and within a given locality. The unexpected reality is that "concepts far" of the outsider can be those of the neighbor, not simply ideas marked by little physical proximity. "Concepts far" bring different eyes to local places, announcing dissimilarity as the way and manner in which one understands and engages differences in daily communicative life.

In this historical moment, the notion of rhetorical interruption takes on a cast akin to the theater of the absurd, placing conventional expectations on their heads. Instead of rhetorical interruption stopping the unreflective bliss of routine, we are more likely to find rhetorical interruption interfering with change, offering a respite, a moment of routine. In this odd moment in which a rhetorical interruption looks more like a moment of calm, a moment akin to the silence before the storm, routine more than change brings forth genuine surprise. In such moments "concepts far" become the concepts of local engagement that begin with difference, not commonality.

In a time of change that moves routine to the unique, we find ourselves within a time of perpetual change, an ongoing journey through the haze, the fog—through a place where one's vision is blurred, at best. In places without the vantage point of assurance of absolute correctness, the task of a philosophy of communication cannot be to predict behavior in an unchanging environment. Rather, the task is to understand how to make sense of environment before us. Philosophies of communication do not render a picture of existential life that calls for duplication or imitation—rather, a given philosophy of communication guides ever so crookedly through the haze before us.

Philosophies of communication are better understood in the words of Hannah Arendt (1994) as *Essays in Understanding*. A philosophy of communication is an essay in understanding. Arendt took this impulse into her dissertation work, which she did on Augustine under the guidance of Karl Jaspers. She considered Augustine to be the first existentialist and understood his work as a "long philosophical discourse on memory" (p. 26). Memory engaged in ongoing shaping of human existence of the "I" in the midst of an existential fog seeks to find temporal clarity. One then begins to pen a philosophy of communication for the existentially short of sight, all of us taking a memory that becomes the present in which the "I" must find its way.

One can see the makings of a philosophy of communication in the life of Arendt herself. A Jewish woman in Nazi Germany and an intellectual, she stated,

> My trouble was that I never wished to belong, not even in Germany, and
> that I therefore had difficulty in understanding the great role which home-
> sickness quite naturally plays among immigrants, especially in the United
> States where national origin, after it lost its political relevance, became
> the strongest bond in society and in private life. (Arendt, 2003, p. 5)

Arendt (1997) wrote in a "modern age" when belonging or the
longing for a sense of belonging dominated, and she offered an alternative—warning us against the power of the parvenu, a person
seduced by the temptation and desire to join and be accepted at any
cost by a group that will forever deny him/her "insider" access to
their social space. The person seeking to join a group rests perpetu-
ally on the outside, with others refusing entrance. Arendt offered
insight into a world in which belonging is not the premiere motiva-
tion; her insights imply the beginnings of a philosophy of communication that has pragmatic implications for a society addicted to the
space Arendt called the "social," a place where individual autonomy
ironically follows the crowd of consensus.

Arendt offers, unknowingly, a pragmatic definition of a philosophy of communication. The phrase "essays in understanding" spins
a web of ideas that moves us to temporal clarity. The following
chapters of philosophy of communication in the everyday offer us
"essays of understanding."

Essays in Understanding

The "Introduction" by Melissa Cook and Annette Holba unites
discussion of philosophy of communication and communication ethics around two major themes: question and presuppositions. They
remind us that each philosophy of communication begins out of response to the historical moment, seeking to respond to a question,
and reflective of the presuppositions that one brings to the response
and to the question. They remind us that a philosophy of communication that meets the everyday is responsive to a question and
makes public the presuppositions that guide the engagement and
temporal clarity from that engagement. A philosophy of communication is a public conceptual map.

"Understanding *Schadenfreude* to Seek an Ethical Response"
by Annette Holba takes us immediately into implications of this
term—finding joy in damage done to others. The implications of
this perverse joy have historically shaped the "dark side" image of

a small town. This reaction to difference takes on the celebratory campaign of hurt toward another. In a postmodern era defined by difference, one might hope such action exists no longer, but studies on mobbing and bullying tell us otherwise. Holba reminds us of the importance of dialectical advocacy dependent on a public forum in which light brings evidence and, over time, separates it from opinion. She reminds us of the necessity of a public space in a philosophy of communication class, not for ideas, but for persons. Philosophy of communication propelled by difference does not end with equal multiplicity, but requires discerning in public light what is worthy of claiming as a temporal set of truths.

"Political Communication and Ethical 'Celebrity Advocacy'" by Melissa Cook takes us to the odd intersection of modernity and postmodernity. Celebrity as advocate is a modern concept of agency. Yet, the hope is to put in place a petite narrative for a given cause. Perhaps the moral of this story is that the origins matter—beginning with modernity ends us with a perverted narrative structure akin to a consumer culture. Cook reminds us that origins matter; the presuppositions shape the outcome.

"Ethical Dialogue in the Classroom" by Rev. John Amankwah suggests that the metaphor of dance works in the dialogic classroom. He reminds us of the historical call of moments in the classroom that we cannot invent, but to which we must respond. Perhaps the most important response is to those moments so far from dialogue that we call them monologue—those moments make dialogue possible at a later time. Our patience for the "without dialogue" makes the learning in dialogue ironically possible.

"Narrative Identity and Public Memory in Morocco" by Fadoua Loudiy makes a contribution with the metaphor of "praxis of public memory." The movement from memory as history to memory as action is central. Reliance on Paul Ricoeur and Hannah Arendt shape the realization that behavior only becomes action when in story form, and memory in praxis is never static history, but an ongoing engagement with the present. Public memory in praxis is the communicative engagement of the extended present.

"Dialogic Meeting: A Constructive Rhetorical Approach to Contemporary Public Relations Practice" by John H. Prellwitz engages public relations as a philosophical communicative ground. He takes the issue of public relations and moves it into interpretive engagement of the historical moment. After reading the chapter, one wants to sign up for a public relations job in order to do philosophy of communication in everyday life. The chapter takes us to the importance of responsiveness to the historical moment and its pragmatic importance for a profession often attentive to telling the story; yet, in this case, the moment shapes the question that the story must engage.

"Narrative Literacy: A Communicative Practice of Interpretation for the Ethical Deliberation of Contentious Organizational Narratives" by Elesha L. Ruminski reminds us of the importance of reading an expansive understanding of the text. She asks us to understand organizational life as a text with an important caveat. What makes a good reader is the content one brings to the task. Reading life in an organization is yet another call for content. The conclusion she takes us toward is not one of process, but the raw necessity of content in the communicative act of reading.

"Dialogue as the Labor of Care: The Necessity of a Unity of Contraries within Interpersonal Communication" by Marie Baker Ohler extends the notion of dialogue into the human condition insights of Hannah Arendt. This work reminds us of words such as labor, burden, toil, and guilt. These are terms not often associated with dialogue, yet are engagements central to Arendt, Emmanuel Levinas, and Martin Buber. Her contribution to dialogic studies is serious in that she moves us from the demand for more dialogue to come to me, to a contrasting communicative act of caring with labor, burden, and guilt that calls forth a dialogue attentive to the Other.

"Engaging the Rhetorical Consciousness of an Organization for Dynamic Communicative Exchange" by S. Alyssa Groom brings the work of Calvin Schrag to the forefront of story construction and telling in an organization. She then connects an organization's rhetorical consciousness to the question, "Does the organization have a story engaged responsively with the historical moment that has both coherence and fidelity that guides both internally and in the meeting of an uncertain set of external circumstances?" The rhetorical consciousness centers on the knowing, the meeting, and the engaging of the story of the ongoing communicative life of an organization. Groom concludes that stories matter and that our ability to tell them responsively matters even more.

A Continuing "Bravo"

The scholars in this volume elicit a "bravo" for taking philosophies of communication into everyday engagement. They offer us no final answers, but they do model what it means to make sense of the mist that obscures clarity of vision that is before us. They give us a taste of philosophy of communication as the intercultural communication of everyday life.

Finally, I offer thanks to this field of study that is so diverse that we sometimes wonder whether we are in the same field of study. What binds us is not methodology, but practical curiosity that Richard Gregg and Julia Wood (1995) framed as the pulse of this field. I offer a "bravo" to the authors of this volume and to a discipline that makes such scholarship possible although moving simultaneously in opposite directions. What a glorious discipline—before the term "postmodern," we were just that. We are not in the field of chaos, but in the field of communicative responsiveness, not from one perspective, but from many. We were the discipline of intellectual narrative and virtue contention long before it was politic to offer such an admission. The authors of this volume are the recipients of this heritage and we the benefactors of a world that the authors and others continue to open in a field called communication.

References

Arendt, H. (1994). *Essays in understanding 1930–1954: Formation, exile, and totalitarianism*. New York: Schocken Books.

———. (1997). *Rahel Varnhagen: The life of a jewess*. Baltimore: Johns Hopkins University Press.

———. (2003). *Responsibility and judgment*. New York: Schocken Books.

Bernstein, R. J. (1983). *Beyond objectivism and relativism: Science, hermeneutics and praxis*. Philadelphia: University of Pennsylvania Press.

Geertz, C. (1973). *The interpretations of cultures*. New York: Basic.

Gregg, R. B., & Wood, J. T. (1995). *Toward the twenty-first century: The future of speech communication*. Cresskill, NJ: Hampton Press.

Contributors

Melissa A. Cook, Co-Editor, is Assistant Professor of Communication in the Department of Communication at St. Vincent College, Latrobe, Pennsylvania. She received her Ph.D. in Rhetoric from Duquesne University. In her classroom, Dr. Cook combines her industry and professonal experience in nonprofit management with her scholarly interests in communication ethics, public relations, and advertising. She teaches communication ethics, interpersonal and organizational communication, advertising, public relations, and political communication.

Annette M. Holba, Co-Editor, is Assistant Professor of Communication Studies in the Communication and Media Studies Department at Plymouth State University, Plymouth, New Hampshire. She received her Ph.D. in Rhetoric from Duquesne University. Dr. Holba has articles published in *World Leisure Journal, Praxis, Cosmos and History: Journal of Social and Natural Philosophy, The Pennsylvania Speech Communication Annual, New Hampshire Journal of Education, Florida Communication Journal,* and *The Hatchet: Journal of Lizzie Borden Studies.* Dr. Holba has a book chapter in *Media(ted) Deviance and Social Otherness: Interrogating Influential Representations* (2007, Cambridge Scholars Publishing) and she is the author of *Handbook for the Humanities Doctoral Student* (2005, PublishAmerica) and *Philosophical Leisure: Recuperative Praxis for Human Communication* (2007, Marquette University Press). Her forthcoming publication is entitled, *Lizzie Borden Took an Axe, or Did She: A Rhetorical Inquiry* (Teneo Press).

Rev. John Amankwah is Assistant Professor of Communication Studies at the College of Mount St. Joseph, Cincinnati, Ohio. He received his Ph.D. in Rhetoric from Duquesne University. Rev. Dr. Amankwah's primary teaching is in the area of Public Speaking, Small Group/Interpersonal Communication/Intercultural/Mass Communication, and Media Studies. His research and professional experience are in communication ethics with primary emphasis on Dialogue. His scholarship focuses on a humanities approach to ethical dialogue driven by a sense of responsibility toward the Other, an approach that privileges the interplay of human relationships within families, communities, and religious denominations, especially in the Catholic Church. Rev. Dr. Amankwah is the author of *Dialogue: The Church and the Voice of the Other* (2007, Peter Lang).

S. Alyssa Groom is Assistant Professor and Undergraduate Director in the Department of Communication & Rhetorical Studies at Duquesne University, Pittsburgh, Pennsylvania. She received her Ph.D. in Rhetoric from Duquesne University. Dr. Groom's teaching, research, and professional experience are in integrated marketing communication and communication ethics. Her scholarship focuses on a humanities approach to integration that privileges the interplay of communication theory and application as integral to strategic integrated marketing communication, organization and brand strategy, and campaign development.

Fadoua Loudiy is a doctoral candidate in Rhetoric at Duquesne University and an instructor at the Department of Communication at Slippery Rock University, Slippery Rock, Pennsylvania. Her dissertation is entitled *Negotiating the Past: Paul Ricoeur and the Rhetoric of Political Reconciliation in Morocco.* Her research interests include the philosophy of communication of Paul Ricoeur, communication ethics, democratization and the rhetoric of political transitions, and intercultural/international communication, with a particular focus on the Middle East and North Africa. She is the co-author of "Testing the Red Lines: On the Liberalization of Speech in Morocco," in *Human Rights Quarterly* 27, 3 (2005): 1069-1119, and author of "Phobias Reborn: Memory and Politics of the Other" in Mark Roberts (ed.), *The Post-9/11 Syndrome.* Albany, NY: State University of New York Press (forthcoming).

Marie Baker Ohler is a lecturer in the Department of Communication at Northern Arizona University, Glendale, Arizona. She received her Ph.D. in Rhetoric from Duquesne University. Dr. Baker primarily teaches Rhetorical Studies, Organizational Communication, Interpersonal Communication, and Communication Ethics. Her scholarly interests include topics such as dialogue, communication ethics, and the use of narrative in creating and maintaining organizational culture.

John H. Prellwitz is Assistant Professor of Communication at the University of Pittsburgh–Greensburg, Pennsylvania. He received his Ph.D. in Rhetoric from Duquesne University. He and Annette Holba have published "Revisiting *Disputatio*: Returning to Dialectic in Debate/Civic Argumentation" in the *Speech Communication Association of Pennsylvania Annual*, Volume LIX (2003): 74-88. Dr. Prellwitz teaches Media Relations, Public Relations and Advertising Strategy & Practice and his research interests include Friedrich Nietzsche, Rhetoric, Dialogue, Mikhail Bakhtin, Communication Ethics, Philosophy of Communication, and Public Relations.

Elesha L. Ruminski is an Assistant Professor of Communication Studies and Coordinator of the Leadership Studies Minor in the Department of Communication Studies at Frostburg State University, Frostburg, Maryland. She received her Ph.D. in Rhetoric from Duquesne University. Dr. Ruminski teaches Rhetorical Studies, Organizational Communication, Conflict Management, Leadership Studies, and Women's Studies. Her scholarly interests include gender politics, communication ethics, rhetorical analysis of the recruitment of women into the International Brotherhood of Teamsters union, and pedagogical and ethical issues of teaching in a wireless network environment.

Index